Shadow Work

Work

A Guided Spiritual Journey Through Healing for Beginners

(Unleash Your Authentic Self and Discover the Secrets of Your Inner Exploration)

James Dorgan

Published By **Kate Sanders**

James Dorgan

All Rights Reserved

Shadow Work: A Guided Spiritual Journey Through Healing for Beginners (Unleash Your Authentic Self and Discover the Secrets of Your Inner Exploration)

ISBN 978-1-7774070-8-7

No part of this guidebook shall be reproduced in any form without permission in writing from the publisher except in the case of brief quotations embodied in critical articles or reviews.

Legal & Disclaimer

The information contained in this book is not designed to replace or take the place of any form of medicine or professional medical advice. The information in this book has been provided for educational & entertainment purposes only.

The information contained in this book has been compiled from sources deemed reliable, and it is accurate to the best of the Author's knowledge; however, the Author cannot guarantee its accuracy and validity and cannot be held liable for any errors or omissions. Changes are periodically made to this book. You must consult your doctor or get professional medical advice before using any of the suggested remedies, techniques, or information in this book.

Upon using the information contained in this book, you agree to hold harmless the Author from and against any damages, costs, and expenses, including any legal fees potentially resulting from the application of any of the information provided by this guide. This disclaimer applies to any damages or injury caused by the use and application, whether directly or indirectly, of any advice or information presented, whether for breach of contract, tort, negligence, personal injury, criminal intent, or under any other cause of action.

You agree to accept all risks of using the information presented inside this book. You need to consult a professional medical practitioner in order to ensure you are both able and healthy enough to participate in this program.

Table Of Contents

Chapter 1: The Dawning Light On Shadows 1

Chapter 2: The Feminine Silenced 15

Chapter 3: The Journey Within 31

Chapter 4: Embracing Sensitivity And Intuition 57

Chapter 5: Crafting Your Feminine Legacy 97

Chapter 6: The Sacred Feminine And Spirituality 121

Chapter 7: Recognizing Fear And Anger 148

Chapter 8: Unearthing The Seeds Of Fear And Anger 153

Chapter 9: The Power Of The Shadow .. 159

Chapter 10: Facing Triggers 176

Chapter 1: The Dawning Light on Shadows

Societal norms have conditioned us to peer all of the above eventualities in a lousy light. We are conditioned to simply accept as true with that tears are a signal of weak point, that emotional expression—specifically from women—is a sign of bad self-control, that seeking to address a extra conventional function in the domestic is laziness, and that stereotypical femininity is a sign of decrease intelligence.

From a more youthful age, society suggests us that female trends are weaker than masculine trends. We are knowledgeable now not to cry, no longer to show worry, now not to specific our ache, and to be robust. We are categorized crybaby, wuss, difficult, or touchy. These labels all deliver a horrible implication, and most humans would possibly do whatever to keep away from being called these things. I recognize you probably have a listing of labels that you in no manner need to be achieved to you. For me, it changed into girly. I grew up in a community wherein all our play became difficult and more masculine. Being popular thru pals depended on your capability to maintain again tears regardless of how tough you acquire hit.

And I have become actual at it. I cherished it once I became the handiest individual who didn't cry regardless of how tough the video games had been given. I have become happy while we had been punished at college and I modified into the fine one which didn't bend to the instructor's will. I'd serve out my punishment with a quiet remedy as it supposed I will be the chief of the group. It meant being a reduce above my buddies.

By the time I end up in my 20s, I felt conflicted approximately who I became. I preferred to dress up. I preferred to cry. I favored to show human beings that their phrases harm me. I favored on the manner to release all of the darkness inner me. But I emerge as frightened of being referred to as girly, prone, or sensitive.

I'd used those phrases in competition to considered one of a type girls, and I became afraid. Afraid that I'd lose all credibility in the international. And this have come to be my 2nd of popularity. It have grow to be obvious that I actually have grow to be no longer happy with my lifestyles. I modified into now not taking factor within the existence I had carved out. I had boxed myself in, and the field have emerge as choking the lifestyles out of me.

As I looked for a way out, I observed out that my testimonies had been no longer as specific as my fears led me to keep in mind. I became simply one of the tens of hundreds of thousands of women trapped inside the global's suppression of femininity. I modified into both a victim and a perpetrator. Society's defective notion of "girl inclined point" had guided me into the field, and I actually have come to be actively perpetuating this perception via looking for to field distinct girls in.

This hobby drove me to do a little factor I'd in no way finished in advance than— look deeper into myself. And the discovery became each enlightening and painful. Decades of conditioning had have become me blind to my personal self. I located out that I had no concept who I in reality emerge as. My reaction to life felt extra like practiced choreography than a real expression of my real self. Something needed to change.

The Shadow

The "shadow" is a term coined with the resource of manner of Carl Jung, a Swiss psychiatrist and psychoanalyst. In his intellectual approach, Jung believed that the essential factor to attaining nicely-being and turning into whole changed into to mix all factors of our personalities in desire to simply focusing on the signs and symptoms and signs presented. The cause of the Jungian method is to create wholeness within the person, an integration of the aware and the subconscious additives of who we are.

So, what does this propose?

At the number one level, we have were given the components of ourselves that we gift to the world and the additives that we hold hidden. And every now and then, we don't disguise the ones elements on motive. We are unaware that we even do that. We suppress the factors that we don't like, and try to simplest show the components we deem "well."

However, this technique fractures who we're. We turn out to be overwhelmed thru tension, fear, shame, or possibly anger while the ones components display up. We decide others harshly based totally totally on the factors of ourselves we don't like, which makes us experience worse, no longer better. Unfortunately, despite the truth that we do our extremely good to hide those "awful" components, they constantly have an impact on our lives, relationships, and capacity to like and take transport of ourselves. Suppressing those elements draws us further and further from who we certainly are.

The time period shadow refers to the elements of our personality that we suppress, reject, repress, or are ashamed of.

According to Carl Jung, actual recovery simplest turns into viable at the same time as we integrate our aware and unconscious selves. Who we in reality are is a sum of the mild and dark components of our personalities, and we cannot benefit self-interest until we assimilate the dark components in preference to distancing ourselves from them.

Rachael was certainly one of my correct friends in university. She became easy-spoken, glad-go-fortunate, and wonderfully conscientious. When we first met, I turned into continually in awe of her apparently clean method to existence. It wasn't till we got closer that I noticed the ache at the back of the grins and the concern at the back of the difficult artwork. She have emerge as so scared of humans locating out about her an awful lot tons less-than-exceptional home existence that she created a facade she knew humans would like. But as her roommate, I come to be aware about the bouts of anger, the expression of low vanity, the constant requests for reassurance, and the self-hatred that determined her screw ups.

I changed into moreover suffering with my demons at the time, so we had been a perfect pair. We'd faux it in public, then wreck down collectively behind the curtain. However, we'd each experience so guilty for breaking down that we ended up spiraling. And this turn out to be how we made it into treatment.

The components we conceal from the sector are a part of who we're. They do now not depart clearly because of the reality we keep them hidden. And Jung recognized that. He understood that those hidden additives had to come to mild, to be widespread, in advance than we determined out our real selves.

What is Shadow Work?

Shadow paintings is essentially the tool of assimilating your shadow so that you can come to be complete once more. Shadow art work entails three critical steps:

1. Identifying and acknowledging your shadow.

2. Analyzing and confronting the shadow.

3. Accepting the shadow.

Shadow art work may sound like an easy pastime, but it's far disruptive. Shadow artwork calls on you to impeach the fame quo (your life as you realise it), damage down your walls and boundaries, and make friends with the additives of your self that you have been repressing and maintaining off for who is privy to how long.

Because of its disruptive nature, shadow paintings isn't always for absolutely everyone. Shadow art work requires handling heavy truths, feelings, and truely, factors of ourselves that we'd as an alternative now not meet. Because of this, shadow work commonly feels worse in advance than it receives better.

This way that the manner might also make you query your lifestyles, and bring up ugly truths and overwhelming feelings. To make it thru the difficult instances and advantage healing, you need to have a maintain near on yourself. You want to be able to speak yourself down from the ledge, to stop your self from being crushed, and everyday, a way of controlling yourself.

This makes it a tough practice for a few, including individuals who enjoy:

depression

insomnia

trauma

anxiety

low vanity

acute intellectual health problems

Essentially, in case you without issues lose manipulate and get lost on your thoughts and feelings, embarking on shadow paintings want to no longer be step one. First, you need to prioritize managing the problems you face so you can expand wholesome coping conduct and beautify your capability to deal with topics that threaten your self-identification.

If you continue to want to begin shadow work, prioritize seeking out professional help. With the assist of a educated expert, you'll have the crucial help to create a recovery plan so as to have a sturdy guide device to guide and prevent you from going too a long way, too speedy.

Shadow artwork requires whole honesty, so don't deny your gift situation and stress your self to embark on this adventure in case you're now not as much as it. There's no shame in acknowledging which you aren't organized.

So, if you are exceptional that this is the right path, and you're organized, permit's begin with a simple exercise. The first step of shadow work is acknowledging the shadow, and this begins with the useful resource of figuring out your shadow. This exercising uses reminiscence and storytelling to find out a shadow. We'll find out more techniques within the subsequent financial disaster, so use this exercising as a way of having organized for the heavier obligations coming your way.

Shadow Work: Relevance and Implications for the Modern Woman

At its center, shadow paintings is a deep dive into the darkest elements of ourselves. It is an excavation, bringing to light matters that would were hidden for many years. This is tough for lots motives, but mainly it threatens to disrupt the reputation quo of our lifestyles.

For many ladies, a social masks has been the everlasting fixture of their lives. We live in a society that requires us to be sturdy in instances that require vulnerability. We are pressured to prove why our thoughts want to be heard, to conform to society's expectancies of who we are purported to be, to name out injustices without displaying strong emotional reactions, and to wear many hats genuinely to make sure the consolation of others over ourselves.

As we navigate over the years looking to take a look at societal standards and private expectations, we lose ourselves within the fray. The corporations we find out ourselves in moreover area high-quality strain on who we're alleged to be and how we're supposed to act. As we navigate numerous circles, we put on mask that agree to the expectancies of those agencies.

At artwork, we comply with the environment we are in. I recall certainly one of my colleagues once I worked as a server in a restaurant. We were within the same high college, and on the time she had been a boisterous, loud, expressive, and honest individual. I loved without a doubt how she'd stroll right right into a room and make every person sense seen and heard.

Chapter 2: The Feminine Silenced

I do not know why femininity wants to be associated with vulnerable factor. Women need to be loose to particular who they may be without thinking, 'I need to behave like a person, or I want to tone it all of the manner right all the way down to gain fulfillment.' That's a top notch manner to maintain ladies down

The suppression of femininity is not a current day phenomenon. Misogyny, sexism, and sexual violence are all motives—and effects—of woman suppression. Even as we champion the reintegration of femininity at the person and collective stage, we appear to inadvertently silence varieties of femininity that don't healthy the mould.

What do I suggest? Well, feminism commenced out as a manner to champion the rights of girls. To supply ladies a boost in a society that has profited off their backs at the equal time as nevertheless denying them identical rights and reimbursement.

However, feminism itself nevertheless fails to incorporate each shape of lady expression. Because the combat for equal rights requires aggression, tough conversations, and dogged tenacity, these masculine developments have inadvertently end up part of the feminist movement, lots in order that greater female inclinations and historically girl roles are avoided within the movement.

The silencing of the girl is finished via both the allies and the warring parties, which in addition suppresses the expression of femininity. This makes it hard for us to really take delivery of our femininity, as we are though conditioned to recall that femininity is synonymous with inclined thing.

The Suppression of Feminine Qualities—A Historical Exploration

Take a 2d to remember the fate of women in the beyond. What includes mind? Most folks right away think of early marriages, compelled marriages, and systematic oppression. And at the same time as this is actual, our statistics books constantly skip over a few critical things—the girls who made top notch strides in records. There have been lady philosophers in historic Greece, however we in no manner have been given to have a study them due to the reality ancient documentation overlooked them.

But lady suppression goes past the erasure of lady ancient contributions. It is likewise very lots present in our presentation of statistics. For instance, at the same time as we bear in mind medieval Europe, we be given as actual with that women had been in reality handled as assets and a manner for the family to consistent riches, electricity, and characteristic an impact on. We moreover see the ladies as silent sufferers in all the topics that took place to them. However, the truth is that this changed into only applicable to the girls within the higher social schooling. The ladies in the decrease social instructions had been energetic and loose. They labored in severa industries, together with masonry and smithing.

They had been caretakers and vendors, at the same time as their rights were seen as nonexistent. With the Age of Revolution, but, the upward thrust of the center elegance saw extra women being treated as property as their families sought to garner extra power and upward push through the education.

However, suppression of the female is a worldwide phenomenon, one which has been happening because historic instances. While researchers agree that feminine suppression takes area, there are conflicting reasons supplied. Some maintain that woman suppression is a end result of way of life, others keep that capitalism is guilty, whilst others kingdom that patriarchy is the primary wrongdoer. Others, rightfully so, blame faith. They are all right. These elements all play a factor inside the demonization and subsequent suppression of the woman.

The intersection of religion and subculture in feminine suppression is obvious in the exercising of widow suicide. Confucian and Hindu cultures in China, Korea, Indonesia, and India considered widow suicide because the notable manifestation of chastity for the bereaved partner, consort, or retainer. This exercise have come to be based mostly on the concern and tension that a widowed lady need to transgress sexually at any time. Sexual expression in girls turn out to be taken into consideration a weak spot and a deliver of disgrace. With no husband to restriction her, the widowed girl modified into considered a ticking time bomb. No comparable exercise existed for widowers.

Multiple religions and cultures perpetuate the fake narrative that girls are inclined and can best be allowed to exist underneath the rule of thumb of thumb of guys. The transgressions of fellows are often omitted, with ladies bearing the brunt of the blame.

Honor killing, through manner of the usage of definition, is the homicide of a girl or woman with the aid of male people of her own family. Honor killings, which may be almost always excused the use of spiritual motives, are also based on lifestyle. Honor killings usually contain fornication or adultery, but rarely are the men worried held answerable for their element.

In early Christianity, women accomplished a key detail within the growth of the religion. Christianity had a greater kind of women, who were instrumental within the humanitarian sports of the church within the community. They fed the terrible, taught lessons, opened hospitals, and ran orphanages. The better-magnificence ladies who had been concerned in the ones sports activities have been mainly criticized for blending with the horrific and advised to forestall the sports.

However, because the religion grew and won greater electricity, girls have been vilified. While they had been though walking orphanages, the selection-making have grow to be stripped from them. They provided the hard paintings however have been demonized as temptresses, and their preference-making competencies have been undermined.

The ancient oppression of the lady may additionally additionally seem too brutal, but a few organizations although have abhorrent practices geared toward suppressing woman sexual expression. In 2023, 15% of ladies and women aged among 15 and 49 were circumcised in Kenya (Sheikh, Cheptum & Mageto, 2023). Female Genital Mutilation (FGM) is executed in some groups in Africa, the Middle East, and Asia. Practitioners agree with that FGM controls lady sexuality and complements the male's delight.

The suppression of girl features has labored to maintain ladies complicit of their suffering. By believing that their inherent features are proof of vulnerable point, women are bogged down thru disgrace and guilt, which continues their spirits broken. Because of the worldwide experience of feminine suppression and the prevailing belief that "as a minimum it's not as horrible as in _____," developing above the suppression has been a journey that has however to be acquired.

With such a lot of factors contributing to the relentless suppression of the female, it becomes tough to absolutely loose each girl. However, it is possible to upward push above the suppression as an character and to help exceptional girls see the mild.

The Psychological and Emotional Repercussions of Suppression

The collective and man or woman suppression of real trends, masculine or female, has a tremendous effect on each the person and the community. In this phase, we'll interest at the consequences of lady suppression at the character.

At its center, suppression limits the freedom of expression of an individual. Some dispositions which can be taken into consideration stereotypically woman embody nurturing, expressiveness, humility, passiveness, kindness, tenderness, emotional expression, warm temperature, naivety, and lots of others.

For some readers, truly analyzing some of those tendencies may additionally additionally furthermore elicit an emotional reaction. If it does, take a second to notice the emotion and the trait that motives the reaction.

Exercise 2: Identifying Triggers

You can carry out this workout at this thing, or after reading via the rest of the financial disaster. This exercise desires to use emotive language to find out which tendencies are possibly part of your shadow.

We commonly have a tendency to instinctively react to suppressed dispositions, and this exercise is aimed inside the direction of assisting you pick out tendencies which might be part of your shadow through tracking your emotional reaction.

Please communicate to Exercise 2 within the workbook for further commands.

When we suppress critical elements of our identities, we limit our freedom of expression and deny ourselves the chance to correct and trade any volatile tendencies. This consistent suppression has a wonderful impact on our intellectual and emotional fitness, and those troubles appear through:

Hypervigilance—When your shadow manifests itself abruptly, specially with terrible results, you're left thinking even as it's going to take region all all over again.

You emerge as constantly aware of your phrases and moves, tracking how you react to keep away from getting stuck off shield once more. This hypervigilance is not healthful, as it keeps you disturbing and sick comfortable in each situation. It maintains you repressing your manifested shadow in choice to diving deeper into it to remedy the scenario.

Anxiety—Repressing elements of yourself which you are ashamed of will constantly motive anxiety while you discover your self in situations wherein the trait has a bent to take vicinity. If you commonly commonly generally tend to cry while you're accused falsely—that is a viable, sincere reaction—you can continually revel in stressful while you encounter a comparable situation. You don't even want to be accused of feeling irritating. If the situation took place at a store, you'll commonly sense demanding while you step into the store, or even as you see the individual that accused you.

Denial—We will be predisposed to take top notch measures to disclaim the additives of ourselves we pick out to live hidden. Even even as we're faced with proof of the manifestation of our shadows, rarely will we admit that it is part of who we are. We are quick accountable the possibility individual or the scenario in preference to recognizing the conduct for what it's far—a manifestation of a hidden a part of ourselves.

Numbing—To what quantity do you visit avoid uncomfortable feelings and triggers? Numbing is one of the common responses to pain, and it generally includes convincing your self that you aren't brought on with the resource of the situation. In intense situations, drugs and substances turn out to be the numbing sellers. Numbing similarly represses the traits being averted, which makes the state of affairs marginally worse.

Stress—Our repressed tendencies are nonetheless part of us, or even while we maintain them locked down and out of sight, we're never comfy. As we repress greater tendencies and connected emotions, our stress degrees frequently boom. We may not moreover be aware about the developing pressure stages, but the results of everyday pressure constantly appear in a unmarried way or each different.

Projection—This is a common protection mechanism, one which attempts to distance us from our shadows. Projection includes attributing our private shadow to another individual. We may additionally get induced thru a confident man or woman and accuse them of vanity due to the fact we're denying our vanity. Projection tries to change the script responsible one-of-a-kind people while the problem lies with us. Projection keeps us from bringing our shadow to mild, which allows the repression to maintain uninhibited.

Depression—Repression prevents us from nicely expressing our emotions and responding to situations as it should be, leaving us saddled with trapped emotional electricity, which no longer frequently entails terrific responses. The loss of expression leaves us feeling trapped in our our bodies, and this results in melancholy, as we are crushed through the weight of our very private repressed emotions and thoughts. Because there may be no reprieve in the out of doors worldwide, we sink deeper into despair, glad that we have no unique preference

Behavior repetition—The manifestation of our shadow is more regularly than not subconscious, and a few people by no means understand how their shadow manifests. Because of this, we repeat positive behaviors without even noticing. By repressing the traits, we respond in wonderful methods while we find ourselves in situations that motive our shadow. Defense mechanisms are essentially repeated responses to such conditions.

Irritability—Repressed feelings entice energy interior us, giving us no outlet. This places us on element, specially in interactions with different human beings. We are with out problems angered or feel positioned out even as we're dealing with mild inconveniences, or while matters don't pass our manner. When we are constantly on aspect, we are an awful lot much less tolerant of people and situations, and we start drawing close to conditions with pessimism. This will boom our hypervigilance and pressure ranges.

Chapter 3: The Journey Within

The adventure of integrating your shadow to find out your actual self takes place in tears. First, you need to acknowledge the lifestyles of your shadow. Second, you need to discover the trends which can be contained within your shadow. Finally, you want to discover the records of these tendencies, and consequently, how your shadow emerged.

Many humans discover it mainly difficult to make it via step one as human beings, we satisfaction ourselves on being ideal. We want to accept as true within our goodness and distinctive feature. We mistakenly expect that acknowledging our shadow is admitting our faults.

The pain of admitting our mistakes, faults, and shortcomings is every now and then an excessive amount of to go through, and in a few instances, mainly painful. So, at the same time as we're first confronted by using the fact of our shortcomings, it turns into a whole lot less difficult to sink returned into what we're used to—hiding the darkness. We find out it plenty less complex to run a long manner from the truth in desire to dealing with it. The comfort of our comfortable lack of facts is good to the fact of our real selves. We count on we're happier believing in our goodness, however this does not anything to make the happiness a reality.

To without a doubt consist of the happiness of our real selves, we've got got to overcome our want to bury our heads inside the sand as regards to our shadows and the tendencies inner. We have on the manner to sit down within the ache of our undesired traits and so that you can hold uncovering them.

A Woman's Journey into Her Psyche

Uncovering what we opt to continue to be hidden is a hard manner, however one that wants to be embarked on if we're to emerge as our actual selves. To begin this manner, we first want to look deeper into ourselves—deep sufficient that we're capable of see the elements interior our shadow. Introspection, or self-mirrored image, is vital in the adventure of integrating your shadow to benefit wholeness.

Introspection manner taking the time to study your self. To find out, and rediscover, who you surely are. Who are you? What are your desires? What are your desires? What drives you? Why do you behave the manner you do? How did your contemporary-day self come approximately? Who do you need to be?

These might probably appear to be smooth questions to reply, however whilst you dig deeper, you will be amazed by using the use of the answers that resonate with you. Introspection in shadow paintings serves a selected purpose—to attract out your shadow and to find out the manner it came to be. Introspection offers you a hazard to face your shadow with aim and empathy. It is not approximately calling out your "bad" trends, however assisting you notice yourself for who you virtually are.

For instance, if you are as an alternative important of your self and others, introspection does now not call on the manner to simply list this trait. It is prepared locating out why your internal voice is specifically vital, and which conditions, inclinations, and those motive the worst of the judgment. Introspection, therefore, turns into an prolonged-term gadget. Your shadow is a cease result of repressed inclinations, emotions, and conduct, and some can be more complex to remedy than others. So, as you begin your introspection journey, you want to technique it with staying energy. Do no longer try and force a leap ahead.

Exercise 3: Let's Explore

Your individual is a give up end result of the dispositions, behaviors, and emotions you've publicly and privately expressed. When beginning your introspection adventure, diving into the deep surrender may want to make you protective, undermining the achievement of the adventure even in advance than it has commenced out. In this exercising, we are able to adopt a clean cruise thru who you're. You are unfastened to adopt this workout as regularly as you want or add extra gadgets to the list if you please.

All I ask is that you stay honest. And in case you face any hassle, please file it.

Please talk over with Exercise 3 within the workbook for further commands.

Introspection keeps us aware about our internal worldwide, assisting us understand who we're and why we are the way we are. This self-attention isn't most effective useful to our existence, growth, and recovery, however it moreover allows us to navigate the arena without adding to others' burdens.

Have you ever had the pride, or displeasure, of managing a person who is ignorant of themselves? They generally tend to make the lives of anybody round them hard with out noticing or being concerned. When they get referred to as out, they're brief to play the victim, putting blame on all of us and the entirety however their behavior.

Introspection saves us from being this man or woman. It permits us to appearance our behavior, to upward thrust above our ego's defensiveness, and attempt toward recuperation. Introspection is a center a part of shadow paintings and the subsequent recuperation. Practicing the above workout with relative frequency allows us to discover ways to be greater honest with ourselves and to get comfortable confronting our shadow trends with out resorting to unhealthy coping conduct.

Healing the Wounds

Digging through the beyond is an critical a part of shadow art work because it facilitates you discover the start of your ache. By information why you're the manner you are, you may determine the way to cope with the developments which are constantly inflicting you pain. Your emotional and mental health are surely as crucial as your physical fitness, although shadow art work can also involve residing through pain as a part of the healing way.

Introspection is absolutely a part of the equation with regards to recovery. Awareness with out in addition motion leaves you in the same area. To make a difference, cognizance desires to be complemented thru way of steps inside the direction of restoration.

In this section, we'll find out restoration actions which might be clean to adopt. However, this doesn't mean that the manner can be pain-unfastened. You will want to be unabashedly honest with yourself and organized to are looking for help at the same time as you feel beaten.

Our pleasure has a way of masquerading as a protector of our well-being while in reality it serves as an impediment to recuperation. So, if you revel in similar to the following healing channels are not operating for you, or in case you come across an great emotional reaction, don't permit your pride save you you from looking for help. Shadow artwork is supposed to be painful and tough, no longer debilitating. You want to nevertheless be capable of function in life at the same time as you approach tough feelings.

If your existence is carefully impacted thru shadow art work and the whole lot goes out of types, SEEK HELP. Don't permit your pleasure to jeopardize your healing.

Journaling

As a healing device, journaling is a awesome exercise that may be customized to serve whichever reason you want within the period in-between. The sporting activities we've got blanketed to this point are all variations of journaling. In shadow paintings, journaling is a discovery and healing tool. As a restoration tool, it may be used to:

shed mild at the tendencies that need without delay addressing.

carry out a chunk blind exploration whilst you're uncertain of the purpose of your pain or unease.

technique sports, emotions, mind, and hurts in a stable vicinity.

document styles that can be used to discover shadow developments, triggers, or obstacles to restoration.

reframe computerized thoughts and feelings with more beneficial, balanced ones.

file your recovery development over the years.

file your exquisite tendencies as you combat negative, self-critical beliefs.

The above examples are certainly a place to begin; you can use the Companion Journal in any manner you need, as lengthy because it enables you in your quest for recuperation.

Journaling is an easy workout to begin, however maintaining it may be tough, specially even as you begin shining a mild at the shadow inclinations you'd as an opportunity continue to be hidden. As with all practices, you want to start small. Don't try to cram your entire healing technique into some durations.

You want to start with the small topics so you can bring together get hold of as true with to your power and show yourself a few goodwill. By bringing the an awful lot a lot less horrific dispositions into the slight and integrating them into your manifested character, you sense more confident tackling the greater damaging ones.

To turn journaling right right into a addiction:

Set up a devoted region and time for practice—A ordinary is the great way to jumpstart a addiction. The area can definitely be a chair or perhaps your bed. Choose a quiet time while you could take a seat down collectively along with your thoughts without distraction. However, don't select a time that requires you to start a very new addiction.

For instance, in case you awaken at 7 a.M., don't pressure your self to awaken at 6 a.M. So you may mag. Instead, pick to mag proper now upon waking up and pre-plan one part of your morning everyday. For example, choose out your clothes the previous night time and use those 5 minutes to magazine. With time, you could awaken a piece earlier to encompass an extended journaling consultation. You also can pick out out to mag as your coffee is brewing or choose out clean, no-prepare dinner breakfasts so you can lessen out the cooking time.

Always have your Companion Journal handy—There might be moments of impromptu breakthroughs or realizations. Having your mag or your digital notebook to be had can help you file moments or mind which might be vital or illuminating.

This is specifically vital in case you are nonetheless inside the shadow discovery section of your restoration journey. By documenting an event or a idea, you can set aside time later inside the day to technique the state of affairs, feelings, or mind to higher apprehend yourself and what you need to better cope with a comparable scenario.

Set up a journaling template—Free-shape journaling is a effective exploration and processing technique in healing, however it may be hard to make use of it correctly at the same time as you're truely beginning. A journaling template will assist you recognize what you want to recognition on, stopping you from going deeper than you could deal with as you're genuinely beginning.

A journaling template is only a series of turns on that jumpstart your meditated photo session. A clean set of activates implements the WHAT, WHY, WHEN, and HOW questions. These questions although will let you allow your thoughts and emotions drift freely at the equal time as supporting you reputation on a specific detail of your journey at a time.

This shape is straightforward:

What: What befell? This query highlights the problem with a purpose to be tackled. Are you documenting a idea, feeling, behavior, or state of affairs? This is a report of the shadow trait being added to mild.

Why: This refers to the existing state of affairs. Do you have got were given an concept why you had that particular notion, feeling, or response? Or why the situation opened up because it did? This query is great close to figuring out triggers.

When: The timing additionally may be vital. If viable, constantly be conscious at the same time as the perception, response, feeling, or situation transpired. It doesn't need to be the time, however the widespread context is ok, e.G. During my morning commute, in the meeting, or the bathe.

How: This is a preemptive recovery approach that pursuits to help you recognize your coping competencies. How do I cope with this? In this segment, provide your mind on a way to address the manifested shadow trait. This isn't about being proper or incorrect, however approximately know-how your answer patterns. You don't need to place into impact this advised answer at once as it is able to be a defective knee-jerk response.

Once you have got got the state of affairs said, it is time for mirrored picture. This is wherein the second one why is to be had in. In the mirrored photo, discover the motives why you answered to the scenario in that way. This is the exploration of the reasons behind the manifestation of your shadow trait. Once you've got got explored why, evaluate your how and decide in case your solution ought to though have a look at.

Exercise four: The Healing Journal

This exercising is aimed in the direction of supporting you higher apprehend the journaling template described above.

Please speak over with Exercise 4 in the workbook for further commands.

Set aside one session for examine—Shadow paintings is a non-forestall system of increase, and you want to be aware about your improvement. Reviewing your magazine entries is an essential part of measuring your development through the years and figuring out kinds of behavior, mind, and triggers.

You can choose out to record your assessment in the Companion Journal or a 2d journal, to have the ability that will help you with lengthy-time period progress monitoring. Ensure which you set apart adequate time to your look at consultation considering that your introspection may be spanning severa entries which may cover precise shadow trends and techniques you employed to deal with said trends.

Never skip the examine, even if your entries all hobby on one trait or reason.

Allow your mind to glide freely— Journaling is about baring your soul on paper. While your prompts can also furthermore pressure you to attention on a particular subject matter, your description isn't always constrained. Allow your mind to allow cross of the whole lot approximately the state of affairs. Do not stress your self to put in writing in a particular manner, to apply correct grammar or maybe legible handwriting. When you begin self-improving your entries, you're sure to additionally edit the state of affairs and forestall the invention manner.

Write all of it out because it comes. Note even the seemingly minute info that don't appear connected. Within these phrases is the reality, which turns into obtrusive as you examine thru them or on the same time as you write.

Always remind your self why—Journaling for healing gets difficult. It gets painful. Your magazine is a documentation of factors you've been retaining hidden, consciously and unconsciously. By bringing them to slight, you are certain to shake your existence. You mess with the manner subjects turned into once and pressure yourself from your comfort region. And even as we get uncomfortable, we fight to go back to the norm. To the way subjects become, despite the truth that it wasn't walking out.

When you start journaling, write your "why" on the duvet web page. What is the prevent motive? You can choose out a quick-term motive and a long-time period one. The goal is to heal, whether or not this includes restoration from trauma, coping with tough persona tendencies, or maybe self-attention. When the exercise gets hard, remind yourself why it's far critical. You may additionally even take a look at your evaluation magazine if you need encouragement to maintain going. While keeping the workout going can be hard, quitting is a great deal worse.

Meditation

Just like journaling, meditation is a practice that can be tailor-made that will help you address superb dreams at super times. As part of shadow paintings, meditation is a exercising that allows you to become familiar together together with your shadow. It offers you a danger to sit down down with the shadow without denying or suppressing its lifestyles. Shadow meditation targets that will help you discover ways to get maintain of your shadow with out judgment, to experience the ache with out feeling the need to run away, and to encompass the shadow, ultimately integrating it to become your real self.

If you've explored the arena of meditation before, you are aware about mindfulness meditation. If you haven't, permit's discover what it's far, as this paperwork the muse of shadow meditation.

Mindfulness Meditation

Mindfulness meditation is a exercising that seeks to bring your hobby to the now, the triumphing 2d. It is a way of drawing your interest and interest in your bodily, emotional, and non secular state at that second. Unlike mirrored photograph, mindfulness meditation is set announcement, not judgment or rationalization. It is listening to the thoughts that bypass via your mind, your emotional response to those thoughts, and the manner your frame feels, from head to toe.

Mindfulness meditation is a remarkable foundation for shadow meditation because it acclimates you to the practice of non-judgment. As you exercise mindfulness meditation, you get used to sitting collectively with your feelings and mind with out trying to change them or repress them. Mindfulness meditation encapsulates each your brilliant and terrible components and works to create a famous self-attention of who you are. When you are used to this, sitting collectively along with your shadow will become a touch bit less difficult with greater exercise.

Exercise 5: A Mindful Session

This exercise is geared in the direction of assisting you jumpstart your meditation exercising. We'll recognition on mindfulness meditation as it's far the precursor to shadow meditation.

Please take a look at with Exercise five in the workbook for similarly instructions.

Building your mindfulness meditation training to encompass your shadow artwork consists of intentionality. Before starting your session, set your reason for the consultation. Your first few periods may be committed to shadow area. That is, the ones are scouting periods aimed towards locating your shadow. Having the ones commands allows you to turn out to be familiar with deliberately searching out pain.

When you can discover one shadow trait, a few sessions may be dedicated to calling forth and sitting with the feelings which can be added forth by using the use of the trait. However, your motive isn't always a "want to get up." What do I suggest? Your purpose is a proposal, not a rule. If you meant to take a seat with an emotion however it's miles too overwhelming throughout the session, it's miles ok to just reputation to your breathing and enjoyable. This isn't a failure. It is a discovery of your contemporary limits.

The purpose is to befriend your shadow through calm recognition. Fighting your feelings will now not attain this. When you strain your self to sit down with an emotion, it jeopardizes your practice. You will unconsciously start to associate meditation with overwhelming pain, pushing you to surrender on the exercising to keep away from this pain. So, take it sluggish and admire your limits.

Exercise 6: Shadow Meditation for Beginners

Shadow meditation is a very intentional exercising aimed toward bringing forth uncomfortable, and once in a while painful, thoughts and emotions. This meditation leans into the basis that our emotions are beacons of our us of a of being. Our feelings are honest reactions to mind, feelings, and conditions. We can also try to hide and repress them, but this honesty in no way fades. So, shadow meditation leans into the feelings we've regarding certain components of who we're, and with the resource of processing and accepting these feelings, we ultimately take shipping of those components of ourselves.

This workout is aimed closer to supporting you discover ways to comprise shadow meditation into your mindfulness meditation workout effectively.

Guided Imagery

Guided imagery for shadow work consists of visualization into shadow paintings meditation, consisting of a brand new measurement to the workout to make it greater effective. Guided imagery, basically, is a recovery device geared in the direction of helping humans collect targeted rest. It's a meditative device that engages the senses to create effective scenes that stimulate the body's herbal relaxation response.

But, isn't shadow paintings an exploration of the uncomfortable and painful? The solution is certain. However, this doesn't advocate that you cannot create a more accommodating area for your mind that will help you interact those uncomfortable and painful emotions. Guided imagery locations you in an area in that you experience snug and strong. This way, you can infuse the ones emotions of consolation and peace into the shadow tendencies which you discover sooner or later of the meditation session.

Chapter 4: Embracing Sensitivity And Intuition

Women, and guys, everywhere in the worldwide recognize that being labeled "too sensitive" isn't supposed as a reward. It is an expression supposed to indicate susceptible point, which we take transport of as it seems to be a shared sentiment in the course of genders and generations. Children who are susceptible to crying are avoided early by their friends, categorised crybabies, and more regularly than not, suggested to prevent crying.

When a lady expresses herself with tears in her eyes and her voice cracking, she is a lot less probable to be taken appreciably. A guy within the same scenario He is sure to be mocked for being a [redacted]. You can likely fill in multiple phrases there, none of them effective.

In workspaces, we see ladies paintings hard to show that they're no longer emotional. To avoid being punished for expressing emotion, they have got makeup kits equipped, run to the rest room to cry with their voices muffled, and preserve of their anger in the face of injustice. In worse situations, we're forced to overlook the pain of our colleagues, friends, and customers due to the fact our empathetic reaction will jeopardize our positions. We are conditioned to area accurate judgment first, even supposing the great judgment fails the humans it is meant to help.

But, as studies shows, shunning sensitivity and glorifying bloodless rationality is costing us. Unable to express those emotions, we are compelled to repress them, causing a crack in our psyche. By keeping tears, anger, empathy, and recognition hostage, we trap energy inner ourselves, and the expression, whilst it in the long run comes, is typically explosive and misguided.

For our personal sake and others', we want to override the societal conditioning that vilifies sensitivity. Instead, we want to have a study how sensitivity and intuition make us better human beings. We want to look beyond the slim, warped lens society arms us. We want to appearance sensitivity as an expression of emotional, mental, and innovative electricity.

Challenging Societal Misconceptions approximately Sensitivity as a Weakness

Instead of tackling sensitivity as a well-known idea, we'll spotlight the developments that society lays out to expose us why being touchy is weak. The consensus fails to look the splendor that lies within those traits. I am now not announcing that there are not any downsides to the ones trends, but they are no longer as lousy as society dreams us to consider. After all, even the dispositions which might be taken into consideration "admirable" have their disadvantage. So, why have to we take delivery of as real with society's opinion rather than taking time to appearance deeper?

Sensitive people cherish/crave affection

I don't have any concept even as it befell, but come what might also moreover trying to be desired or loved has become synonymous with vulnerable point in our society. Especially if this sentiment is expressed via a lady. When The Tinder Swindler aired in February 2022, it speedy became a heat subject matter. People were quick to slam the girls for falling for a scammer.

What the ones people forgot, but, emerge as that limitless love scams are perpetuated everywhere in the global, and the sufferers are every males and females. Craving affection is a part of being human, however due to the reality sensitive human beings tend to cherish the love they achieve, they earn the derogatory label "simps."

However, this manner of seeing matters fails to apprehend surely how effective affection makes us. We turn out to be higher humans even as we revel in giant, cherished, and cherished. And there's not whatever as adorable as having your affection reciprocated and favored. While craving affection places you prone to being taken advantage of, this is not a weak point. The fault lies with the person that decides to apply affection to govern and damage the opposite person.

Sensitive people "take subjects too in my opinion"

This is probably the maximum common motive used to justify equating sensitivity to vulnerable point. When bashing sensitivity as a weakness, people will constantly thing to the tears, anger, or severe emotional response displayed by means of manner of the touchy individual. In some conditions, the individual can also had been the intention of hurtful words disguised as jokes or had their insecurities broadcast, and when they reacted, the alternative celebration can be short to call it a "comic story" or label them as "party poopers."

However, on this type of state of affairs, the person who needs to do better is the nice casting stones. Why? Because they overlook the exchange in expression inside the touchy individual because of the reality they fail to apprehend who they're able to make such jokes with and who they could't, and in the end because of the reality it's far smooth their emotional intelligence is underdeveloped.

I am now not denying that internalizing feedback made by means of others is a common trait in sensitive humans. However, in maximum of the instances I've witnessed, the shipping of the criticisms themselves made a distinction. When touchy people are condemned for "taking topics too for my part," the condemners continually forget about that there may be a 2nd factor to the interplay. What changed into stated? How become it said? What have become the emotional reputation of the character expressing grievance?

The touchy person's reaction is sometimes approximately how they made the opposite character revel in, and that hits tougher. So, taking matters in my opinion is a individual quirk, not a weak point.

However, studying to split oneself from the criticism is vital regardless.

Sensitive people are indecisive

Indecision isn't always constrained to sensitive humans. Sensitive humans will be predisposed to take time to make picks due to the truth they may be more likely to bear in mind more additives of the scenario. Because they normally will be inclined to have greater sensory input, they take greater assessing the outcomes based totally on all of the information they have got.

This makes their options more whole, but in a few instances, it's miles a problem. However, this isn't always a awful trait in itself. And definitely not a susceptible factor. Wanting to keep in mind the general ramifications of a desire is admirable, as not many human beings try this.

Sensitive people get too caught up inside the statistics

A sensitive man or woman is more likely to get caught up within the facts because they will be inclined to look more in a situation. Because of their acute attunement to themselves, others, and their surroundings, they be aware diffused shifts and data that may not be obtrusive to others.

In most situations, that could be a superb trait. However, they might wander off within the info and forget the larger photograph, specifically in the event that they've perfectionist inclinations. This isn't always a susceptible point. It can be an inconvenience to organization people while there are time constraints or brief movement is wanted, however it's far continuously higher to be meticulous than shoddy.

Sensitive people are pushovers

This is a not unusual misconception because of a easy truth—pushovers are typically categorised emotional while they are looking to particular their grievances. Being a pushover is often a manifestation of low self-esteem and the selection to be commonplace and loved. They erroneously take shipping of as actual with that they could most effective get affection and reputation inside the event that they take a look at the goals of the alternative birthday celebration.

In worse conditions, the individual is conditioned to recollect this through emotional and physical abuse. They were informed time and time all over again that they are no longer surely well worth it, and that they may be terrific useful once they do what they will be informed. But there's pleasant a lot it is simple to take. When they are trying to invite for better treatment, they may be classified "sensitive" and "too emotional."

Pushovers aren't vulnerable. Sensitive folks who are browbeaten into following others' needs to get hold of popularity and affection are not susceptible. They are people who need unconditional love and recognition. They are folks that want to find out their way into their very very personal suppressed and repressed electricity. They are folks who need to have a take a look at that they'll be powerful sufficient to face on their personal.

Sensitive human beings "get too emotionally invested"

Sensitive humans are some of the maximum emotionally expressive people. Their emotional responses are unbelievably honest, and blended with their high empathy, they commonly have a tendency to get without problems invested in conditions, collectively with fictional ones. They find out it clean to region themselves within the unique party's shoes, every now and then with extra emotional expression than the affected party. This is because of the fact as they empathize with the opportunity birthday party, additionally they get drowned in sympathy and the bias of the situation.

While once in a while they may be capable of skip overboard with their reaction, it isn't a weak spot. It is a testament to their capacity to see the opportunity birthday party really, some thing the region is desperately in need of.

Just because of the truth the sector celebrates and hails emotional suppression, common sense, and apathy does now not make sensitivity a susceptible factor. Many human beings in the worldwide are negatively laid low with the coldness of the world and are desperately looking for someone to just accept, apprehend, and love them. Empathy, kindness, and sensitivity are dispositions which are essential on this global if we want to make it a better vicinity. As Maya Angelou so rather placed it, "People will neglect what you said, humans will forget about about what you probable did, however people will never forget the way you made them revel in."

Celebrating Intuition: The Dance of Vulnerability

Our lives are made from the selections we make along the way, and the manner we make those choices does no longer comply with the same sample all the time. Some of the instinctive picks we make now may not were instinctive in advance than the moves have become ordinary. Think about the primary time you did your laundry.

You have been possibly extra intentional with the hobby than you're now.

As we get used to positive sports via repetition, our brains usually tend to automate these sports activities in order that they don't devour as an entire lot mind energy as earlier than. Additionally, we will be predisposed to carry them out semi-consciously. As we amass more information approximately the world spherical us and automate an increasing number of moves, our unconscious thoughts is likewise accumulating facts. And this is the inspiration of our intuitive expertise.

We visit instinct as a "feeling" or "gut feeling." We recognize some thing, but can't deliver an cause in the back of how. We make a desire however can't give an explanation for why that preference felt right at the same time due to the fact the opportunity one didn't. Even even though intuitive alternatives appear to stand up in a cut up 2nd, they draw upon a wealth of statistics saved in our subconscious and conscious minds. But... this isn't to say that our instinct is a hundred% proper. There are moments while our intuition fails us, however this isn't always not unusual.

Despite this, we're taught to depend more on the rational thoughts, especially as women. When we point out "gut feeling," we are advocated no longer to make "emotional choices." However, men are celebrated for following their intestine instincts. But this need not be a deterrent. Our intuition is part of who we are, a group of who we had been, who we are, and who we're able to be. And trusting our instinct is a big a part of turning into entire.

Our instinct grows more potent on the same time as we're greater open and honest while we technique our emotions with out resorting to repression. We commonly generally tend to subconsciously be conscious styles and acquire records at the same time as we aren't busy hiding from the area. When we fear showing part of ourselves, our interactions are spent in shielding mode, and we now not often look at the subjects around us. This restricted view of the sector additionally impacts how we make selections, and trusting our instincts becomes difficult.

Following our instinct is an expression of our agree with in ourselves, which can be difficult if we are used to bottling our feelings and taking note of internal and societal criticisms. Choosing to boom our intuition requires us to embody our vulnerability and upward push above our fears.

Choosing to encompass our vulnerability is not a vulnerable component. Rather, it's miles a formidable choice considering the reality that you'll be dealing with components of yourself which you'd as an opportunity cowl. And this is why selecting to be prone is an vital step in shadow artwork. So, in which can we start?

1. Allow yourself to be you— Unfortunately, loads parents have mask that we located on relying on the state of affairs or business company. When we emerge as so used to setting on masks, we lose ourselves more and more. We determine ourselves and cover factors of ourselves we count on people will pick out. However, that is certainly self-repression that further hides your real self—from your self and the location.

Accepting your self—flaws and all—and being your proper self, is a volatile bypass. We camouflage ourselves due to the reality we want to healthy in, and via the usage of displaying the arena our actual selves, we chance rejection. And this is why being your actual self is an exercise in vulnerability. You are inclined to show the sector the components of you which you have been hiding, trusting that you may discover splendor.

2. Remind your self of your "why"—It is straightforward to fall lower returned into your antique patterns if you can't recollect why you are selecting change. What is motivating you to take the chance on yourself? Reminding your self why you selected to interrupt a ways from your antique styles and become extra open and sincere will become your source of energy on the equal time as it seems less complicated to simply disguise all over again.

three. Don't save you gaining knowledge of more approximately yourself—We in no way save you finding out new subjects approximately ourselves. From our thoughts, reactions, motivations, and capabilities. When we're busy hiding, we by no means take some time to look ourselves for who we're, and who we may be. When we take the threat and pick to appearance and display our actual selves, we turn out to be privy to more factors of ourselves as they display up.

When we take shipping of ourselves, our shadow inclinations—further to different beautiful tendencies—begin acting. We end up a haven of love for our repressed self, and at the same time as she shows up, we start locating out the depths of our non-public emotions, talents, and motivations. Self-exploration is a lifelong exercise, and also you'll constantly be amazed at how you change over the years.

four. Embrace self-interest in preference to self-criticism—Somehow, we find out it less difficult to decide ourselves in place of accepting ourselves. It is dubious why this is, however self-grievance destroys our trust in ourselves, turning inconveniences into tragedies in our minds.

Instead of criticizing our movements, mind, and terms, how approximately turning into curious? Self-interest adopts an open-mind mentality, on the identical time as self-complaint is a closed-thoughts mentality. When you're curious approximately why you acted, belief, or communicated in a certain manner, you open your international. Self-hobby lets in you to see greater of yourself and your worldwide, even as self-criticism locks you inner random beliefs and misconceptions.

However, self-interest will show you factors of yourself you'd as a substitute have stored hidden, so constantly stay on defend because of the truth those are moments while self-complaint will rear its ugly head yet again.

five. Indulge in new topics and critiques—This is one of the awesome methods to learn how to encompass your vulnerability. The worry of failure is a few element every body revel in to various stages. Even in phrases of fun sports, failing seems to be unwelcome. By attempting new topics, you located your self in an surroundings in which the end end result is unknown.

The need to constantly win is an ego response, and vulnerability requires not heeding our ego's desires of perfection and achievement. Depending on which hobby you pick out to strive, the lessons you observe will vary. For instance, if it's miles a today's ability, you need to depend upon a person else to reveal you the manner. In a set pastime, you want to be cushty with being the inclined link as you research the ropes. By getting snug with now not expertise, it will become less complex to without a doubt accept your flaws and attain out for assist even as you want it.

6. Practice self-compassion—You can't name for recognition from others in case you can not obtain your self. We are often short to show compassion to others however grow to be self-crucial even as we make mistakes, or even think that we did. I'm effective you've got a chum or acquaintance whose quirks you have got were given have been given come to simply accept. "That's how he/she is," you tell others while this individual reacts in a advantageous manner. But why don't you do the equal?

Why are your quirks and mistakes more extreme than those of others? Self-compassion is hard because it calls for us to be sincere about ourselves, to look our faults, and in spite of the reality that be given ourselves. Self-compassion calls for us to prevent turning a blind eye and to be honest approximately our moves, emotions, and mind. And this is an act of vulnerability, as we threat rejecting ourselves and falling over again into the antique types of repression and self-complaint.

7. Become a splendid deal much less involved with what others suppose—We live in a community. No rely wherein we are, we cannot escape associating with exclusive humans, right away or indirectly. And in case you don't already recognise—there may be no manner you may please the hundreds. The human beings round you also are limited via their personal stories, biases, and conditioning. This is the dimensions they will use for his or her observation approximately their very private lives, and yours. However, you need to undergo in mind that nobody will take obligation on your nicely-being. Even

as they shell out advice, they will in no way take responsibility for the recommendation if topics don't schooling consultation.

This is why you need to clear out others' evaluations. I acquired't ask you to tune all of it out, because of the reality a few people do have reviews which can be virtually really worth listening to. But this is the minority, and you want to parent out who's behind the brilliant critiques. The rest of the time, but, you want to simply accept as true with your self greater than you accept as authentic with others. You need to apprehend that exceptional you have got were given your very very very own tremendous interest at coronary coronary heart, as you are the most effective one which knows what you are residing through. So, filter out the noise and pick out yourself. You also can grow to be a nonconformist, but even then, you could in the long run locate your tribe.

eight. Learn to really accept—We make bigger our shadow due to the actions we take to avoid who we genuinely are. Denial is a huge part of repression and suppression, and as a notable deal as it may create completely satisfied lack of expertise, this does not ultimate. The first step in getting any form of selection is acknowledgment. However, surely being conscious is in no way sufficient. Acceptance drives the technique, as we want to just accept that there can be a hassle earlier than we employ techniques to resolve the problem.

But recognition isn't easy. We discover it difficult to clearly take delivery of that we have been wrong. People visit improbable lengths to coloration themselves as sufferers at the same time as they may be the perpetrators. And while faced with this, many hold playing sufferer, deflecting the situation. Acceptance is a powerful device in shadow paintings, and it calls on us to widely known our vulnerability. Accept the conditions on hand and your feature. Learn to peer your actual contribution, and not the self-defensive narrative your ego creates to make you revel in higher.

Acceptance is strong, and it demands admitting the coolest and the unpleasant.

9. Do it anyway—Fear maintains us small. It holds us hostage and continues our shadow growing. When we repress our feelings, it's miles fear that drives us. Fear of going thru our real selves, fear of consequences, and worry of rejection. We don't try new subjects due to the priority of failure. We worry vulnerability due to the truth we anticipate it makes us vulnerable, and this continues us from

coming across new topics approximately ourselves.

The solution is not to be reckless in picks. Rather, the answer is to experience fear and but take a bounce. Even as you experience fear, take a step. Allow yourself to strive first. Trust your power and competencies.

Our vulnerability connects us to our real selves. We get to dive into who we are, and this fosters a connection between our outside and inner worlds. As we find our genuine selves trait through using trait, we end up greater in music with our thoughts, emotions, and reactions. We find it lots much less tough to truly take delivery of our shadow and reconcile our knowledge of ourselves with our real selves, fueling self-popularity, self-love, and intuitive power.

Accepting our vulnerability isn't always a weak point. It is our manner of starting our actual selves to the area and experiencing our lives without the barrier of fear, faulty conditioning, and repression.

The Feminine Unleashed

Embodied internal femininity are vulnerability, instinct, creativity, reflected photo, and compassion. The expression of those tendencies is typically mischaracterized as susceptible point thru society's lenses, and as girls, we discover ourselves doing our outstanding not to show the ones inclinations in sure contexts. Even through the expression of creativity, we strive our nice to break up ourselves from quintessentially lady sports activities sports.

Unleashing our femininity is not an explosive, high-power prevalence, but a gradual reputation that our femininity is our electricity. This consciousness births a modern-day generation in which we discover ourselves feeling extra, expressing extra, and indulging extra with out the dread that we is probably discovered. We begin loving who we are with out feeling the need to provide an explanation for our motivations or ourselves. We don't combat to be understood, however as an alternative experience a non violent lifestyles in which our contentment and peace of mind become the concern.

Have you ever decided your self seeking to provide an cause of why you need something? Or why you don't like something? Trying to justify your tastes to others is disturbing, and it has a tendency to sour the delight of said interest or element. You start noticing flaws, feeling annoyed, and every so often, even ashamed.

Getting returned this delight is viable, however it's miles an intentional way that calls for reminding yourself of the splendor you determined earlier than. This is the identical with our femininity. When a compassionate man or woman is taken advantage of, it hurts. They may additionally vow to in no manner bear in thoughts once more, but hardening their coronary heart hurts them extra than in the occasion that they decided on to forgive and go together with the go with the flow on.

When we give up on our femininity due to the truth society deems it prone, we don't end up liberated. Rather, we wilt in the confines of society's arbitrary pointers. We emerge as a shell of ourselves. True liberation is expressing our femininity for our very personal sake—for our freedom, peace of thoughts, and contented lifestyles.

Accepting and expressing your femininity way:

Getting snug with self-mirrored image. Delving deeper into your self to understand your motivations, likes, dislikes, goals, and hopes is an crucial part of femininity.

Becoming more emotionally expressive. Please don't confuse this with an emotional response. Emotion expression isn't always the knee-jerk response that gets us into trouble. Rather, it's far your emotional response to the scenario available, which may additionally include on foot away and revisiting the hassle once the extraordinarily charged emotions have cooled off.

Allowing your self innovative expression, regardless of what this means that to you. It can be trying new recipes, new books, writing, painting, or drawing. Whatever it may be, your progressive pursuits are an expression of your hobbies and a source of stress comfort.

Prioritizing rest actually as hundreds as you cost productiveness. Downtime is critical for rejuvenation and a damage from productivity fatigue. Taking time to do now not whatever maintains you going for a long time with out breaking down.

Take time to reconnect together with your body. Get to comprehend your frame with care and love, embracing every detail with notable thoughts and compassion. Thank your frame for assisting you carry out every day responsibilities, and constantly purpose to cope with it with the honor and adore it merits.

Taking time to immerse your self in nature, or herbal elements. Nature has a way of grounding us, reminding us of the splendor of life. If a stroll inside the park or a hike thru the woods is not possible, immersing yourself in the tub or taking a relaxing bathe is enough to floor you.

Embracing kindness and compassion. Allow your humanity to shine via. We are brief to select, condemn, and blame ourselves and others. Kindness and compassion are uncommon on this worldwide, at a time even as we want them the maximum. So, be the blessing people want in their lives, and don't forget about to show your self the same compassion and kindness you unfold into the area.

Becoming receptive. We usually have a tendency to keep away from soliciting for assist because of the reality we count on it makes us susceptible at the same time as this is not the case. Giving is extremely good, however so is receiving. Receiving method you upward thrust past your pleasure and ego and be for the reason that you may't do it on my own. It method spotting and acknowledging your shortcomings and selecting to attract at the electricity of some exclusive man or woman. Independence is terrific and all, however don't drown due to the reality you're afraid to name for assist.

Embracing collaboration. Joining fingers with others to perform some trouble is a plus for everybody concerned. Society likes pushing the "self-made" time desk, however that is in no way feasible, mainly with large wins. No you could do it all by myself. Collaboration allows definitely each person to pool their strengths, regardless of the interest. So, permit go of the want to do all of it your self and consist of the power of the humans with you.

Allowing yourself to transform. Femininity requires self-splendor, but this doesn't advise settling into elements of your self that aren't running out. Transformation is an essential a part of femininity. The insights of your self-reflected image are not just bits of records to store away. Rather, they are guides for your transformation. They assist display you what you want to work at once to emerge as your fine self.

Activating your femininity is a go decrease back on your proper self, but there is greater to the approach if you want to build up a non violent, balanced existence. Femininity is one-half of of of the dual energies that exist inner us. Embracing your woman side isn't a name to suppress the a bargain-celebrated masculine aspect. This will keep you off stability and suffering to feel entire. Balance is accomplished with the resource of embracing your masculine and lady energies. You can be at peace while you receive your manifestations of each energies, now not even as you fight to be one or the alternative.

Masculine vs. Feminine the Balance Required

This e book is an exploration of the splendor of femininity and its role in shadow paintings. However, this does not suggest that female electricity is the best energy you need to awareness on. The exploration to this point has been to help you recognize the price of femininity for your life. And simply as treasured is masculine strength. We all have both energies inside us, and prioritizing one over the possibility reasons chaos and imbalance in our life. Why? Because the expression of each masculine and girl strength, to diverse degrees, is critical in unique situations Activating your femininity is not a call to forget about approximately approximately your masculinity. Rather, it's far a name to pursue stability.

However, please phrase that this stability isn't always a 50/50 expression of both energy. The expression of every electricity is determined with the aid of the scenario, this means that that that the expression is severa. For instance, being impulsive at some stage in your loose time is incredible, however this gained't be first rate at art work. Kindness is brilliant, however whilst you recognise someone is taking gain of your kindness, assertively setting up barriers is what is going to bring you peace.

When there may be an imbalance among the energies, you're bound to:

experience stuck

revel in disconnected

warfare with choice-making

Self-pondered photograph and self-compassion can help you stay in tune in conjunction with your internal and external global, which helps you to understand the right energy to cope with the situation reachable. Let's find out a few opposing yet complementary masculine and woman developments.

Emotibility vs. Rationality

This is possibly the most important difference this is delivered up in the direction of femininity. However, there are moments whilst emotional response wins over rationality. For example, showing compassion to a harm toddler is higher than telling them how they went wrong in that state of affairs. By presenting kindness, you permit the right now situation to loosen up. You can later discover the state of affairs rationally even as you want to train them why they shouldn't repeat the actions.

Emotional expressions have their area, and information that is an expression of emotional intelligence.

In the same vein, there are moments whilst rationality wins over emotional expression. If there may be an emergency at artwork, crying and panicking fail to address the state of affairs. However, assessing the scenario and locating techniques to deal with the problem is the proper detail to do. The emotional breakdown can come later, as quickly due to the fact the emergency has been handled.

Impulse vs. Structure

Schedules, policies, and structures dictate such a variety of facets of our lives that it's easy to sense limited. Spontaneity is fun, glad, and releasing. However, there may be a time for each. If you've labored or teamed up with a person who in no way follows any of the set pointers, you understand the way disturbing it's miles. Children whose mother and father are spontaneous and amusing may be the envy of their pals, however as they develop up, you listen the kids say that they choice there has been greater structure within the home.

The balance of masculinity and femininity is understanding that there may be an area for impulsivity and an area for form. It is type to comply with pointers at art work to avoid growing useless troubles at artwork. And it's miles type to get into your vehicle and pressure to help clear your mind on a random Tuesday night time time.

Chapter 5: Crafting Your Feminine Legacy

Somehow, we are capable of find it the stability among who we wish to be and who we want to be. But for now, we in reality ought to be glad with who we're. – Brandon Sanderson

Carl Jung's shadow isn't always an entity that exists in a vacuum. Rather, it's miles one of the 4 maximum vital archetypes that he provided to offer an reason behind the individual. These 4 archetypes, in turn, interact with each excellent in severa methods, growing greater archetypes.

According to Jung, an archetype is a collection of tendencies that create a individual. However, undergo in thoughts that the person does not one hundred% belong to a selected archetype, as we commonly have dispositions and dispositions that fall into unique archetypes.

Jung's 4 critical archetypes are (McLeod, 2023):

Persona—This is the persona we located in public. This is the mask we located directly to experience well-known into our surroundings. It is what we do and say to healthful within the social norms or social settings we are in in the period in-between. This persona, as we've said, isn't our authentic self. It is the fruits of social have an impact on, repressed feelings, and fear of exclusion.

Shadow—The shadow is the dark facet of our psyche. It includes the topics we conceal away and repress in our quest to wholesome into the society we stay in and our idea of who we are. This ebook is prepared healing the shadow so we are able to stay extra healthful lives. The shadow brings us ache as it represents additives of ourselves that we reject.

Anima/Animus—The anima is how the male psyche views the lady while the animus is how the girl psyche perspectives the masculine. These are the mind you have got for your mind approximately what masculinity represents and the jobs of the masculine, and vice versa. The anima/animus is a manifestation of societal and private notions approximately the jobs of the girl and masculine, and it typically pertains to gender roles. The anima/animus partly explains why we generally generally tend to reject and overlook the masculine and female strength based totally on gender. For instance, a lady insisting that the husband is liable for supplying or the husband insisting that the partner is accountable for elevating the youngsters.

Self—This is who we truely are while we reconcile our conscious and subconscious developments. This is what we reason to obtain whilst we adopt shadow paintings—individuation.

From the ones 4 archetypes rise up many greater, however we'll discover the 12 not unusual archetypes on this section. These are the principle archetypes in which most dad and mom fall, despite the fact that a few tendencies can be part of unique archetypes. Exploring the 12 archetypes will assist you find your dominant archetype, and that could be a remarkable manner to select out out your shadows and visualize your real self.

Myths and Archetypes

1. The Innocent

The innocent is an sincere character driven via using their revel in of morality and justice. Their purpose is to stay a joyous and harmonious existence, and that they continuously see the awesome in others. They are honest, reliable, and positive, continuously striving to appearance the best in each situation.

However, the harmless are naive, searching beforehand to the same loyalty and honesty from others. They believe too with out troubles and are without problem disillusioned at the equal time as others don't stay as plenty as their values. However, they're masters of denial, often refusing to face the problems evident at them, as a substitute naively believing that acknowledging the problem will by using a few method make it paintings. They withstand change and are prone to take silly dangers, usually following someone they remember they recall.

They are a pleasure to be round and may be inspiring, despite the fact that their naivety gets them in too much hassle; and this may be disturbing for someone who clearly has their quality hobby at coronary coronary heart.

2. The Orphan

The orphan is pushed via acceptance and connection, and if those aren't to be had, survival. The orphan's largest worry is abandonment, and they'll go to remarkable lengths to keep away from it. Because they crave connection, orphans are very perceptive and empathetic and also are extraordinarily touchy to the reactions of the opportunity character.

Orphans are innovative and hardworking and constantly try and do high-quality in an environment in which they find out recognition and balance. However, if their surroundings is risky, or they nevertheless sense like they don't belong, they may choose to rebel as a manner of rejecting the alternative birthday party first. In worse situations, they will use their trauma as an excuse for his or her horrific behavior, or to control the alternative party into staying.

Orphans also are at risk of being manipulated due to their eagerness to satisfaction.

3. The Hero

Heroes are characterised via the usage of their strength, resilience, and staying electricity, and that is the image people have in mind when they take into account the proper masculine. Heroes are dedicated to their relationships, dreams, and experience of proper or wrong. They are pushed through their task or need to accomplish.

However, they may be obsessive, idealistic, and reckless, particularly of their pursuit of something elusive. They exhibit vanity, mainly in situations in which they revel in like they may be the fine or better than each person else. The hero is sacrificial, but their sacrifice can be jumbled together with the need to be worshiped or visible because the savior.

The hero suggests superb braveness and may typically rely at once to make matters take place.

four. The Caregiver

The caregiver is what people agree with when they visualize the right feminine. Their motivation is to assist others, and they'll be certainly compassionate. Caregivers are generous and selfless, commonly taking up the location of ensuring without a doubt each person round them is taken care of. They are dependable and strong and can commonly don't forget at once to growth a supporting hand.

However, they may be able to with out problem pass from being nurturing to over-concerned. In the extremes, they don't agree with the opportunity man or woman is capable of searching after themselves, even fellow adults. They hover round the rims, meddling at each risk they get.

They can also be overprotective, taking excessive moves of their bid to hold the alternative character secure. The caregiver is also prone to that specialize in others so much they forget about their properly-being. They also are without problems deceived for the reason that they don't take into account the humans they contend with are able to deception.

Their humility is admirable, but the caregiver can without problems come to be disillusioned if the humans round her reject her meddling.

five. The Explorer

Explorers are driven by the use of their hobby and quest for freedom. They live to the beat in their drum, reveling in their place of knowledge. They are fiercely independent and love operating on my own despite the fact that they may be exquisite crew game enthusiasts. They are very supportive of the people they love and typically usually tend to charge colleagues and friends, treating them with excessive apprehend.

Despite their intelligence, they may be flighty and disorderly, inflicting chaos and confusion with out which means to. They may be self-centered, as they spend quite a while of their heads and tending to their very personal goals. This creates a disconnection amongst themselves and others, pushing them in addition into their solitary nature.

Explorers may be gullible because of their immoderate reliance on intuition. They make selections intuitively plenty of times, which makes them clean marks for correctly-crafted manipulation. They might also have problems respecting limitations, each personal and societal.

6. The Rebel

The insurrection's motivation is shaking up the system. The fame quo does now not attraction to them, and they are guided thru the use of their very very very own morality and fee device. However, they live frightened of turning into limited with the resource in their private charge gadget, which could emerge as too inflexible and ensnare them in slim-mindedness.

Rebels are assured, lively, articulate, and decisive, following up on what they have been given all the way all the way down to do with zeal. However, their potential to pursue their want and dreams could cause them to condescending, impolite, and overly judgmental. They can be manipulative and insincere, mainly when they need something from the other person.

7. The Lover

Lovers are altruistic, trusting, and open-minded. They price beauty and respect small pleasures, commonly looking for to find exciting moments to take pride in. The lover is snug with heavy emotions and may take a seat with their emotions. They make extremely good teammates due to the fact they're cooperative, open-minded, and records.

However, lovers usually tend to make selections based totally on their feelings, that could cause them to indecisive and irrational. They are liable to poor emotional regulation, jealousy, anxiety, and depressive signs and symptoms. This is because of their sensitivity to their feelings, which they're in reality on the mercy of.

eight. The Creator

Creators are driven with the resource of their want to create. It doesn't rely wide variety what. They are truely satisfied to be bringing some component into their existence. They are modern-day, passionate, gifted, practical, and modern driven. They will be predisposed to be very impartial and self-conscious. They cost performance and feature a clear experience of cause.

Because in their independence, unmarried-minded awareness, and reason-driven life, they are frequently misunderstood. This locations them at risk of loneliness due to the truth they may alienate people who don't recognize them.

Creators may also moreover placed plenty emphasis on their brilliance and abilities to the aspect of being egotistical and condescending. They have a tendency to be perfectionists and might adopt overcautious dispositions in a bid to supply matters precisely how they want.

If they don't adopt a established, systematic technique of creation, they will fall prey to impulsiveness and chance not finishing tasks at the same time as wished.

nine. The Jester

Charismatic and mischievous, jesters are widely recognized for his or her sense of humor, hobby, and capability to have a look at body language and social cues. They are smart, every now and then too clever for their personal pinnacle. They love making fools out of authority, effortlessly setting themselves in threat of retaliation.

Their carefree thoughts-set is occasionally a natural trait, but every now and then they put on it as a masks to cowl their insecurities and shortcomings. Even even though they're sociable and charismatic, they'll be quite closed off emotionally. They can act recklessly, as they in no way prevent to consider the consequences.

Jesters, specifically if they'll be the usage of humor as a masks, are susceptible to being submissive humans-pleasers. They worry loneliness and exclusion, so they'll maintain up the charade truly to experience blanketed. Wearing humor as a masks is tiresome, and that they will be moody at times.

10. The Sage

Sages are smart, analytical, and rational. They have tremendous essential questioning abilities and are perceptive, which makes them splendid desire-makers. They can separate emotion from reality and discover it easy to certainly accept harsh truths at the same time as final motive. Patient and determined, the sage can be continual in their pastimes, their desire-making competencies boosting their possibilities at achievement.

However, they might become too glad with their abilties and overly crucial of folks who are bogged down through emotions. They are tactless at the same time as criticizing, failing to issue in the emotional reaction of the recipient. Unsympathetic, cold, and isolated, sages are frequently lone rangers.

11. The Magician

Magicians experience the energy of their capabilities, and this fuels their revel in of self-worth. They accept as authentic with in themselves and are driven with the aid of their talents and skills. Rational and smart, they will be pretty perceptive of the area spherical them. They are quite adept at introspection, hardly ever cowering inside the face of their shortcomings.

However, they have got a immoderate capability for detachment, each from their movements and the people round them. If they do no longer rein on this terrible addiction, they may fast come to be isolated.

Magicians are aware of their cleverness, energy, and talents, and this fuels their sense of self-worth. They can become egocentric and conceited, which further alienates them. Despite their excessive revel in of self, the magician has moments of doubt, which fuels their uncertainty. This can disrupt their sense of self if it isn't always successfully resolved.

12. The Ruler

A natural chief, the ruler is charismatic, assertive, and has a commanding presence. Because the popularity quo has a bent to pick out them, rulers experience upholding the guidelines and shape and consider in hierarchies. They are eloquent and feature smooth thoughts and emotions, which they may effects unique with out faltering.

Despite their self notion, rulers are plagued thru the fear of losing their strength and feature at the pinnacle of the ladder in a few thing surroundings they're in. This way that notwithstanding the fact that they take delivery of as proper with in equity, they with out problems lodge to underhanded manner virtually to live in strength. They are domineering and patronizing, especially at the equal time as interacting with people they determine as inclined or incompetent. Goal-oriented and tenacious, rulers are first-rate leaders when they revel in their role is stable.

Please be conscious that no person a hundred% falls into any archetypes. The archetypes are created using the commonplace traits and behaviors placed, but outliers are many. There is a ruler who moreover well-known caregiving conduct. They don't experience comfortable till the human beings round them are adequate. There can be a sage who's so bogged down via their non-public feelings but remains in denial about their irrationality.

By expertise your archetype, you get an concept of in which your shadows generally lie. The weaknesses of the archetypes can be obvious to each person else besides the character showing the behavior, particularly in the event that they body this conduct in extra attractive processes. For instance, a meddling caregiver may additionally moreover furthermore insist that they may be looking after the person in spite of the fact that their conduct crosses private limitations and worse, is beside the aspect.

Understanding your archetype additionally permits you to discover more avenues of self-exploration, wondering even the inclinations you in no manner concept had been expressions of your shadow self. However, as you dig deeper, you could discover that your expressed archetype is a shadow, inclinations that you followed to try to healthful in. For instance, the orphan, who's scared of rejection and not fitting in, also can mask themselves because of the reality the insurrection. They can also reframe their fear of rejection to make it appear like they'll be the ones breaking some distance from the reputation quo. This is a way of covering their fears even as moreover letting them feel find it impossible to resist changed into their preference.

Exploring your archetype is a fun way to start unmasking your shadow with out setting off your alarm bells. Because it starts with the aid of taking a quiz, it will become a amusing game that you could take pleasure in. This manner, you emerge as greater open to sluggish trade.

Sexuality within the Shadows

The shadow feeds off shame in a massive manner. And if there's one element of our lives that's mired in disgrace, it's our sexuality. As women, our our our our bodies are policed plenty, blamed for plenty, chastised, castigated, abused, shamed, and a lot extra.

Sexuality is the device used to achieve these things. Think about it: girls who pick celibacy are shamed for his or her alternatives, and so are sexually expressive ladies. Those who get dressed modestly are truely as at risk of criticism and abuse as people who pick out to revel in their skins.

Religion, schools, society, companies, own family, or maybe buddies all play a element in what sexuality consists of, and thus far, all it has achieved is perpetuate the message that sexuality is some aspect to be ashamed about. This creates the sexual shadow, part of the shadow that plays a huge component in preserving us separated from our genuine selves. Please endure in mind that the sexual shadow isn't always satisfactory approximately the physical trouble of sex. It is also approximately the emotional and spiritual components. What do I endorse?

Let's discover:

The sexual shadow predominantly grows because of the cultural, spiritual, and societal message that sex—and with the aid of manner of extension sexuality—is dirty, a sin, or some thing we want to rid ourselves of.

Sexual desires are condemned, even more so if the ones goals are classified "peculiar." Kinks and fetishes are appeared down on and visible as unpleasant or inappropriate.

Bodies are labeled as "appealing" and "unattractive," which has an effect at the character's experience of self. The media's portrayal of splendor skews the expectations of every men and women and so does the steady moving of beauty requirements.

The above elements have an impact on the emotional trouble of sexuality. Low vanity and the conditioning that the dreams are "ordinary" make it difficult to experience comfortable with intimacy, or to even experience cushty in a single's frame. These emotions of inadequacy and wrongness gas the sexual shadow.

For others, society's double requirements when it comes to sexuality create a totally specific dynamic. The "hookup" culture is quite lots celebrated, but society although pushes for purity, mainly for ladies. So, individuals who crave emotional intimacy may additionally moreover try to reject this a part of their identification to keep away from getting called "prudes" or being rejected through way of someone they decide upon. Others who enjoy bodily intimacy can also additionally furthermore reject the emotional aspect in their sexuality surely to maintain their identity as "easygoing" companions.

In every conditions, the shadow grows because shame and denial play a large function in the manifestation of sexuality.

Sexuality additionally has a spiritual component, which is not always non secular. For some, intimacy is an expression of who they surely are. It is a celebration of lifestyles. However, mainstream spirituality chooses to popularity on one-of-a-kind elements of lifestyles except sexuality.

Chapter 6: The Sacred Feminine And Spirituality

Even as we art work to heal and integrate our shadow selves, we stay a part of the sector. Our each day lives, bodily activities, and relationships are nevertheless active and vital even as we navigate our internal worldwide and are seeking the peace that we deserve. Our femininity is nurtured internally and expressed externally, in which many extra things are competing for our time, hobby, and funding.

When we permit the out of doors worrying situations throw us off course, we lose ourselves inside the fray once more. And if you've been operating on shadow healing and proper expression, you emerge as extra touchy to those modifications once they seem. So, how are we able to find out a way to balance the inner art work we do and our inner international?

Through the adoption of grounding rituals and practices we are crafted from our bodily, emotional, highbrow, and non secular selves, and shadow paintings heals the bodily, emotional, and psychological. Our spiritual increase works to stability out who we are, giving us an area to secure haven and get better.

Spirituality isn't approximately faith. If your faith gives you this stable space, please revel in unfastened to use it as you heal and grow. In this ebook, but, we're able to discover greater modern-day-day spiritual practices that may be followed into spiritual practices or undertaken through themselves.

But first, allow's explore the way to navigate the outdoor global as you determine via embracing and accepting your femininity.

Facing External Expectations

The adjustments you're making on your lifestyles normally have an effect on the humans spherical you, whether or not you want them to or not. Once the ones adjustments begin manifesting, the reactions may be unique relying on how the alternative character is affected. For example, whilst your indignant outbursts and reactions start subsiding, you'll be met with confusion, mainly from people who are closest to you. Because they've placed to live with—and react to—your anger, the absence of stated anger disrupts the popularity quo. They are uncertain whether or not you are changing for the higher or if it's miles a trap.

If you've got were given got been too to be had because of the truth you have been terrified of being abandoned for placing obstacles, showing self belief and assertiveness is probably met thru anger from the ones who have been taking gain of you. The ones who without a doubt care about you'll be careful on the begin, however they'll rejoice your accomplishments after they see you repute up for yourself.

Your former u . S . A . Of being is what others count on of you, and the changes you're making can be met with unhappiness, happiness, criticism, or doubt. The reactions of the humans round you, however tiny they appear, may additionally have a profound effect for your capability to maintain running to your shadow, embody your femininity, and seem your real self. Fortunately, you may nonetheless keep going at the same time as you revel in the annoying conditions of trying to navigate your outdoor worldwide out of your new lens.

Here are some techniques of drawing on your strength to make it through the outside disturbing conditions:

Remind your self "why:" Choosing to discover your femininity and discover yourself modified into not a few thing you decided on a whim. There changed into some factor that emerge as not going for walks to your existence, and also you subsequently chose to change. This is why it's far vital to have your "why" written someplace you may with out issues get right of access to, or to reveal it right into a mantra or confirmation you could recite while your resolve begins offevolved to disappear.

Keep journaling: Your mag is your accomplice on this adventure to your right self. It is a processing device, one which is available in available thru the best instances and the tough ones. When you find out the reactions of humans round you for your mag, you are better capable of approach their phrases and movements. This manner, you may recognize your reactions better, making it less difficult to maintain your solve. Otherwise, you can turn out to be fixated on their phrases and actions and unconsciously revert to the model of your self that they hold calling for.

Stay adaptable/flexible: This is one of the perks of retaining a journaling exercising. As you discover the reactions of people in your environment, you are in a higher intellectual area to discern which statements are unhelpful and which ones are actual concerns. For instance, you may be setting limitations however your approach is dictatorial. That is, your obstacles are one-manner. While your adjustments can be running, you are not always going to get matters right at the number one try.

So, make journaling evaluation a dependancy. It is a notable manner to understand each your inner and outside global. It creates a location wherein you can discover your international with more intentionality, consciousness on what's crucial, and note any elements of your adventure that need a trade in tempo or approach.

Remain aware of your feelings: Your emotional reaction to the arena spherical you is a excellent indicator of your internal recovery development. As you have got interplay with others, you're already aware of how your shadow inclinations display up emotionally. As you heal your shadow self, your emotions remain the best indicator of improvement or lack thereof. By ultimate privy to your emotions, you could pinpoint reactions that signal in which your sore points are in interactions with others, particularly their reactions to your new self.

Find a help systems: Shadow art work is a in massive component man or woman technique, however you still want manual at times. When a person on your circle is aware of what's taking location to your lifestyles, the adjustments you want to make, and the traumatic conditions you are encountering, they turn out to be an satisfactory pal. They become the sounding board whilst you need an ear, the voice of cause at the same time as you want it, and a cheering squad whilst you are making improvement.

Your useful useful resource system is also a first rate manner of information how your changes translate inside the actual worldwide. They assist you understand the reactions others have, and they permit you to stand your ground even as you wobble and revel in like reverting in your vintage self.

Your help machine may be a pal or family member, but this isn't always a have to. Seeking professional help is moreover an desire. In addition to assisting you delve deeper into extra overwhelming shadow tendencies in the healing method, a expert is a super guide device due to the fact they offer purpose insights. This way, you're positive that they are no longer pushing you in a fine course for their gain. A professional makes a exquisite choice if you don't have absolutely everyone to your circle who may be certainly honest with you.

Remind yourself of the rewards: This may be the same as your "why," or it might be specific. Are you influenced thru what you will be escaping or what you may be gaining? Or both? When your cause why doesn't appear sufficient, don't forget what you're jogging closer to. Visualize your pleasant life while you navigate via shadow art work and encompass who you're. There isn't any right or incorrect manner to preserve yourself at the song to restoration. Allow your self to rise above the task inside the way that works for you.

Nurture self-compassion: Self-compassion is an absolute necessity while navigating through the outside global as you're healing. When others are not too type of their remarks approximately your modifications while you're unsure in case you're on the proper course, or even as your development stagnates or lapses, you need to maintain in thoughts to be type to your self. Self-compassion permits you to look past the shadow that is ingesting you. Self-compassion reminds you which you are human, offers you the push to face a difficult time with out condemning yourself, and permits you to drag yourself up over again.

Self-compassion is tremendous in some unspecified time in the future of journaling, sooner or later of restoration, and as you rise up your actual self within the out of doors global. Nurture self-compassion; allow yourself to embody your self with love and facts in preference to criticism and self-loathing. Remember, there may be no reason to make your adventure more difficult for yourself, but there is every purpose to make it easier.

The outdoor international and internal international exist in tandem. While you can choose to explore your recuperation in solitude, your improvement can handiest be measured via your interactions in the outside global. The recommendations above are high-quality for exploring the demanding situations that embody others' expectancies that threaten your healing improvement. You don't want to exercising all of them, however you need to workout intentionality when choosing a way that will help you efficaciously navigate recovery in each your internal and outer worlds.

Emotions—More Than Just "Being Emotional"

This may additionally moreover appear to be an vain repetition, but this is a reminder of the manner crucial your feelings are to the approach of discovering and integrating your shadow developments. Emotions are also the alarm and guiding systems that will help you understand your pain elements further on your healing development.

Learning to apply your emotions as a recovery tool is an intentional practice that calls for staying electricity, self-compassion, and perseverance. As you heal and emerge as better at navigating your emotions in a healthful manner, this does not imply that challenges will disappear. Rather, it manner that you however want to workout warning due to the fact your ego can also come into play with greater intensity than earlier than.

What do I suggest?

As you turn out to be much less reactionary and get higher at expertise your emotional responses, you is probably lulled right right into a experience of consolation and self notion on your abilities. When something takes place and you slip into your vintage reactionary styles, your pleasure may additionally additionally come into play and turn the slip into a few factor massive than it is. Because you have been assured on your emotional fitness, this could be a cause that motives you to spiral deeper into your vintage conduct. Growth and development normally include a hazard—the danger of a perfectionist mind-set. The satisfactory conditions ought to be celebrated, however don't permit them to prop up your ego an excessive amount of.

As you show your emotional development, constantly live aware of your highbrow interpretation of the improvement.

Observe the emotion: You can do that in real-time or in the course of your journaling manner. How you showcase an emotion isn't the equal for distinct human beings, so this assertion is a way of information yourself. Where are you feeling the emotion? How is it manifesting?

Acknowledge the emotion: As it is already manifesting or has manifested, denying the lifestyles of the emotion will excellent jeopardize your recovery and emotional nicely-being. When you react to a state of affairs, it's miles simpler to justify the response than to sit down down with the feeling. By absolutely acknowledging the right emotion answerable for the response, you supply your self a hazard to understand what took place.

Process the emotion: Emotions are communique systems, allowing us to higher recognize what's taking region to us and round us. In your recuperation journey, processing the emotion is a important component of recovery. You need to apprehend why the sports introduced about the specific feelings interior you, and why some conditions are so triggering you react instead of processing the situation first.

This is the maximum extensive element and is generally completed later when topics have calmed down and you could calmly explore the gathering of sports. Processing your emotions is a highbrow and emotional affair, as you want your mind to find out the solutions. It is this a part of the equation that permits you to discover your ache elements—elements of your shadow that you haven't honestly explored or healed but. This is the cause why you may't look faraway from your feelings or trivialize a response.

Integrate the emotion: Even the emotion which you are ashamed of is a part of you. Integrating the emotion approach embracing the emotion as it's miles and the issue it plays. Anger is a part of the style of feelings you could show off, and at the equal time as getting irritated at a clueless little one is shameful, this does not recommend that anger has no place for your existence. Getting irritated at an abuser is valid as it may propel you to do a little component first-class approximately it.

Integrating your emotions reduces your possibilities of treating them as enemies. You apprehend that they're part of who you are and that they have a position to play in your lifestyles. All you may do is adopt wholesome methods of coping with them in region of repression and suppression.

Always be pleased about your emotions due to the fact no matter the fact that the response within the interim turn out to be wrong, it changed into a training 2d. A reminder of the elements of your self that also need work.

In shadow artwork, femininity, and regular nicely-being, the aspiration is displaying emotional responses, no longer emotional reactions. This way allowing yourself a second to understand the situation in advance than formulating a reaction. It is ready taking the "appearance earlier than you leap" technique.

Remember: Your emotions aren't a stumbling block to the manifestation of your real self. They are the publications to your actual self. Allow yourself to experience, and use the emotions to discover who you truely are.

Spiritual Practices

Spirituality isn't synonymous with religion. In this context, religious practices talk over with the sports activities that join you with yourself. As you hook up with yourself, it will become less complex to hook up with your religious ideals, some thing they will be. When you are conflicted and uneasy, your connection to the divine additionally suffers. The turbulence inner becomes a hassle for your herbal connection to your better being.

These practices are smooth and can be used as complementary practices in your one of a kind spiritual practices. These practices name for intentionality and consistency. They are not emergency practices to be undertaken even as times are difficult, however conduct to be fostered.

Meditation

We have explored shadow meditation, which is aimed towards revealing shadow tendencies. As a non secular workout, meditation is a manner of connecting with yourself. There are numerous meditative practices, and there is no right or incorrect meditation practice to encompass. You can practice whichever form of meditation that satisfies your desires at the time.

Meditation may be guided, self-guided, however, or with movement. My advice is to also undertake motion-based totally meditation. Meditative strolling, yoga, Tai Chi, or even aware chores are tremendous meditative sports that may assist with the monotony of quiet, seated meditation.

Meditation pastimes to reconnect with yourself and to calm your mind, body, and soul. This manner, you may see subjects extra definitely, without feelings clouding your perception. You can strive severa sorts of meditation to find the excellent which you are maximum cushty with. Start sluggish, allowing yourself to workout with minimum worrying situations to offer your self better odds of achievement.

Visualization

Visualization is a effective spiritual exercise that allows you to look your great life, reminding you that it is feasible. Visualization focuses your mind on a unmarried factor, and whilst undertaken nicely, it has a chilled, soothing impact on the thoughts and body.

As a spiritual practice, visualization permits you to connect with your proper and sincere desires. By seeing it for your thoughts's eye, you may recognize your goals and right self with greater ease.

Let's explore a easy visualization exercise:

Find a quiet spot in your property and sit down down efficaciously. With your eyes closed, take deep breaths, sinking deeper into the comfort of your area. As your mind quiets down, do not forget your perfect self. How do you appearance? What are you doing? What expression do you've got got were given in your face? Where are you? Who is round you?

Keep building the records. Nothing is without a doubt too small or too big. Once your photo is whole, take a deep breath and be given as real with a bubble of slight protective the photograph. Watch because of the truth the photograph is captured within the bubble, growing smaller and smaller, enough to in shape in the palm of your hand.

Open your palms and watch the bubble flow into your hand. Hold the bubble for a

2nd, then carry and press your palms in opposition on your heart. Feel the bubble to your coronary heart, embracing the immediately with love and pride. Express gratitude to your self for the dream you maintain to your heart.

Take a few deep breaths, open your eyes, and emerge as aware of your surroundings all yet again.

This is best a easy exercise to begin you off, and you've the freedom to tweak the exercising to fit your goals. For instance, having a candle or track to create a snug environment is amazing, and so is selecting a guided visualization exercising. Visualizing permits you to foster preference and assemble resilience, offering you with the fortitude to hold going while topics get tough.

Journaling

The versatility of journaling is extraordinary. Journaling may be used for gratitude, introspection, preference-making, shadow artwork, or storytelling. Journaling may be a way of connecting with yourself and reminding your self of who you're even as topics end up difficult. You can use the Companion Journal to precise your beliefs and to cement your values and truths.

Journaling as a non secular exercise is simply as versatile. You can write about your visualizations, desires, connection to what you keep in thoughts in, and the belongings you want to do to foster the ones connections. However, you want to be careful about the way you adopt journaling, specially within the center of shadow art work.

Schedule your concrete journaling exercising, i.E. Shadow art work or introspection, and feature a dedicated magazine for this; ideally the Companion Journal to this e-book. This is specially important in case you need to show your development. A 2nd mag also can be used in your spiritual well-being. This way the magazine will satisfy your wishes at any time, irrespective of what form the journaling session takes.

Rest

Femininity thrives on rest and relaxation. It is the alternative of the fiery and busy nature of masculinity, that could damage us down if we preserve at it for too lengthy without taking a break. When we are busy, we barely make the effort to catalog our emotions, thoughts, or physical nation. We are centered on constructing and being effective, making it to the next venture and accomplishment. This is why embracing the restorative nature of femininity is critical.

However, you want to recognize that relaxation is supposed to be restorative in this context. We have a tendency to mention we are resting but take pleasure in sports that go away us feeling even extra exhausted, like chores, errands, or binge-looking. When you decide to relaxation, ensure you're spending your moments on topics that depart you feeling clean and revitalized. What are your calming pursuits? Which sports activities depart you feeling easy and greater lively?

I understand a few individuals who hike as it makes them experience lots better. Others virtually take a seat down and examine at home, while others spend time with buddies. Some sports activities may also moreover seem bodily taxing, but the calming restorative effect lets in us to connect extra with ourselves.

Rest is not about sitting and doing not anything. It is prepared refueling your frame, thoughts, and soul.

Self-Care

Self-care is an all-the-time hobby. It is ready immersing your self in moments that keep you calm, safe, and at peace. Self-care is giving yourself moments that bring a grin on your face, delight into your life, and contentment into your life.

You're possibly familiar with the concept of self-care. At first, the movement become centered at the physical element—enjoyable baths, journeys, and consumerism. However, the sentiment has shifted now that it has turn out to be clean that physical self-care as quickly as per week or periodically isn't sufficient. And consumeristic self-care beats the purpose of the workout if in a while you are left stressing out approximately price variety.

Holistic self-care is set prioritizing your intellectual, physical, emotional, and religious fitness. It is a exercising that makes the small matters remember range. Embracing healthy coping conduct, surrounding yourself with individuals who care about you, on foot far from poisonous conditions, and setting healthful boundaries are all instances of self-care. Taking a spa day is rejuvenating, but the satisfaction will now not last in case you're even though in a traumatic environment the relaxation of the time.

Chapter 7: Recognizing Fear And Anger

Welcome to the primary part of your shadow art work adventure. Today, we are able to move into the dark waters of fear and anger, of our most commonplace and effective shadow factors. Fear and anger, even as unaddressed, distort our mind, adjust our behaviors, and throw prolonged shadows on our relationships. However, with the resource of shining the mild of awareness on them, we are capable of begin to recognize and sooner or later integrate those incredible forces, changing them from hidden monsters to allies on our adventure to completeness.

Let us begin with fear. Rather than being a monolithic entity, worry is a chameleon that weaves itself into the material of our lives in endless strategies. It can also whisper tiny fears, inclusive of the chronic worry of failure, or roar with crippling phobias that keep us in our consolation zones. It can turn out to be persistent procrastination, paralyzing us even in advance than we try to take a chance. Fear can disguise itself as perfectionism, causing us to overachieve on the price of our well-being. In relationships, it can purpose possessiveness or jealousy, erecting obstacles in which bridges ought to exist.

Anger, frequently the polar opposite of fear, explodes like a volcano, searing the entirety in its course. It can take place as vocal outbursts, slammed doorways, or clenched fists. It could probably simmer as passive-aggressiveness, polluting the air with unspoken bitterness. Anger can distort our perceptions, making others villains and ourselves sufferers. It can exacerbate disagreements; power cherished ones away, and departs emotional scars. But underneath the outrage is a message—a want for understand, equity, or unmet goals. Recognizing this message is critical to turning anger right into a stress for fantastic change.

Connect These Feelings with Your Story.

Now it's time to awareness inner. Take a second to endure in thoughts your personal research with fear and fury. Can you endure in thoughts a time at the same time as worry stifled your desires or kept you trapped in a function that sapped your pleasure? Perhaps rage as soon as brought about you to mention some detail you later regretted, leaving severe wounds in its wake. Write down those reminiscences, the remarkable facts, and the emotions that live under the surface. This is your particular map, predominant you thru the unknown land of your shadow.

Journal Prompts

Shadow   Prompts   Response

Fear Recall a time while worry held you lower again.

What were you terrified of?

Did it prevent you from taking a hazard, expressing your self, or constructing a connection?

How did it take area on your frame and thoughts?

Write a letter in your fear, expressing your emotions and intentions.

Anger Remember an example when anger hijacked your feelings?

What introduced about it?

Did it lead to a battle or an outburst?

How did it have an impact for your relationships?

Journal approximately the dreams or desires hidden below the anger, exploring opportunity techniques to unique them constructively.

Don't be fearful of ache as you parent with the ones duties. Let yourself sense the priority and anger so that you can parent out wherein they came from and how they have an effect on you. To trade, you want to have the ability to expose your weak point.

Don't neglect that that is best the start of your journey. In the following couple of chapters, we are going to appearance extra intently at wherein worry and anger come from, a manner to cope with them, and finally, a way to liberate the electricity they hold after they come to be a part of our proper selves. Stay tuned, fellow explorer, due to the fact the shadows cover exquisite training which may be simply geared up to be determined and common.

Chapter 8: Unearthing The Seeds Of Fear And Anger

This bankruptcy exhibits the excellent conditions in which recollections of the past, cultural norms, and murmurs of the existing and former generations sow fear and anger.

Let us now turn to Maya and Ethan's tale.

As a younger lady with a progressive spirit, Maya always desired to be a ballerina and perform on big tiers. But the voice of a crucial critic from a dancing presentation she had as a little one stifled her enthusiasm. An overwhelming enjoy of worry enveloped her, casting a pall of uncertainty on the extent. The fear of grievance casts an extended shadow over her unrealized desires, or maybe in private, she hesitates in desire to jumping gracefully.

The touchy little one, Ethan, rode out a hurricane of rage as he become growing up. The vengeance of his father reverberated via the residence, a trait that had been maintained from one era to the following. Ethan placed to enjoy out this emotional hurricane via way of placing up a courageous the the front and keeping his repressed rage below manage, which he may additionally need to unharness at the primary signal of problem.

We can study that our non-public way of lifestyles is capable of planting the seeds of hate and resentment from Maya and Ethan's enjoy. Scarcity, competition, and the relentless strain to be triumphant are problems that permeate our lifestyle. We turn out to be paralysed via fear of failing, so we comply with the norm and play it steady. The rat race, driven by the usage of anger masquerading as ambition, speedy drains us of our strength and reasons us to lose touch with who we surely are.

The echoes of bygone eras may likely likewise loom large over the right here and now. Our emotional environment may be common through manner of unspoken fears, and genetically transmitted patterns of behaviour, and unresolved traumas. When the ghosts of our ancestors' struggles resurface in our minds and hearts, we also can face inexplicable feelings of dread and rage.

The "inner critic," that accusing voice that follows us about like a shadow, and our "defence mechanisms," those subconscious strategies of handling trauma, are each crucial partners on this route. When we get a manage on how the ones forces art work inner folks, we're capable of begin to query their memories and in the end free up ourselves.

Make the Connection to Your Narrative

It is now as much as you to find out your very own historical past. Think approximately those sports activities activities:

Exercise   Response

Childhood Memories   Recall a situation out of your young humans that evoked excessive fear or anger. Who have turn out to be present? What modified into the cause? How did you react? How did those feelings show up for your frame?

Draw a image or write a poem taking pics the essence of that memory. Let your uncooked emotions glide onto the internet page or canvas.

Societal Influences: Identify societal messages that gas your fear or anger. How do the ones messages effect your selections and relationships?

Create a university or write a manifesto hard these proscribing ideals. Imagine a worldwide in which those fears and anxieties now not keep power.

Ancestral Lineage: Explore your circle of relatives records. Were there instances of unprocessed anger or unresolved trauma? How might probably the ones stories have impacted your emotional panorama?

Write a letter in your ancestors, expressing your know-how and presenting forgiveness. This can assist break the cycle and reclaim your very very own emotional strength.

Final Thoughts

Remember, this exploration can be hard, but it's far important if we're to recognize and combine our shadows virtually. As we unearth the roots of worry and anger, we create area for boom, transformation, and the blossoming of our real selves.

In the following bankruptcy, we will delve deeper into the strength of the shadow, exploring how the ones suppressed emotions can preserve untapped functionality for resilience, creativity, or maybe joy. Stay tuned, costly explorer, for the journey is honestly starting.

Chapter 9: The Power Of The Shadow

The shadow's grip is the maximum effective here. Here we are facing a difficult but in the long run releasing reality: our suppressed poor emotions, together with wrath and worry, have a effective, untapped strain that impacts our lives in methods we do no longer constantly anticipate. Not involved, however equipped to encompass this revelation as a effective catalyst for self-improvement.

Energy That Is Both Visible and Endless

Even the most hidden feelings do not absolutely leave. Like embers in a concealed grate, they warmth up from below, every lightly warming or sizzling the area round them, counting on the manipulate performed. For example, if we repress our fears, they'll ground as chronic anxiety, which can also prevent us from acting on our goals as it paralyses us with indecision. It has the capacity to increase social anxiety, which in turn maintains us secluded and makes the comforting prospect of connection seem some distance away.

As if imprisoned, anger lurks inside the shadows, its kinetic strength warping our views and igniting disagreement. As a give up result, we may additionally additionally hurt ourselves by means of way of becoming irritable or maybe adversarial closer to those closest to us, even whilst they may be seeking to assist us. The subtle poisoning of relationships with the resource of the usage of a steady circulate of animosity can take the form of passive aggression. This is only a small sampling of the debilitating tango of suppressed feelings.

Myths and Self-Constructed Barriers

But the shadow has an effect that goes properly beyond what you could see with the bare eye. When suppressed, terrible emotions like wrath and fear can tie us with restricting ideals. The younger lady who have become teased for having massive aspirations can also now experience unfit of success and concentrate the voice of her fears telling her, "Don't even attempt, you can just fail." If a toddler grows up in an indignant circle of relatives, she or he may moreover internalise the message that everybody is out to get them and use their anger as a defence mechanism.

We assemble our private prisons out of those proscribing beliefs that originate in our unprocessed shadows. They limit our freedom of choice, have an impact at the first-rate of our relationships, and prevent us from carrying out our complete ability. However, a glimmer of optimism can be visible on this gloom; it's the risk that those effective forces may be managed, channelled, and used to our benefit in location of our detriment.

Exploring the Path to Enlightenment

We want to recognize the shadow's latent electricity before we are able to release its latent capability. We can use the ones journaling physical video games as beacons of preference:

1. Panic as a Friend: Think about an area wherein you can face your fears with out fear. How does it seem? Can you decipher its message? Compose a letter in your worry, in that you bring your comprehension and readiness to head. How are you able to remodel your worry into knowledge, readiness, or the bravery to head for it?

2. Anger as Fuel: Think lower returned on an occasion at the equal time as you used

your fury in a brilliant way. In what methods did it inspire you to arise for what you accept as true with in, confront unfairness, or defend folks that were willing? Keep a mag detailing times in which you and people round you could benefit from redirecting your anger into proactive measures.

Keep in mind that the shadow is honestly a powerful, unruly power that may be managed. By embracing its power, delving into its roots, and getting to know its power channels, we are able to unencumber ourselves from barriers and enter the brilliance of our actual selves. We will find out concrete methods for overcoming barriers and embracing the reworking strength of shadows in the approaching financial ruin. Keep an eye fixed constant out, in view that real strength and bravado lie in embracing the darkness.

Acknowledging and Accepting: Embracing Your Whole Being

Now is the time to begin making actions within the direction of shadow integration; we're at a crossroads. Recognising and embracing horrible emotions like wrath and worry without passing judgment is the most critical step. The thing isn't to rationalise terrible feelings however to accept or even welcome them as part of the human revel in, to understand their strength, and to find out strategies to apply them to our gain as we are looking for healing.

Exploring the Depths of Introspection

The first component we want to do is take a look at ourselves within the mirror. As we confide in our journals, they come to be relied on confidantes and safe havens for our maximum inclined feelings:

Create a self-portrait of your dread via manner of drawing a face on your magazine. Tell me the color. In what form does it show up? Recognise the existence of your fear and show which you are open to expertise its message with the useful resource of writing a letter to it. In spite of your fears, how can you emerge as extra courageous and resilient?

Furious Resonances: Think again on a 2nd whilst your fury flared up. Let your fury out in a circulate-of-awareness piece on your journal; do not worry approximately what top notch human beings think. After then, take a step another time and investigate the problem. What spark off the fury? What vital need or need come to be it looking to deliver?

This is not an workout in self-flagellation; instead, it's miles a exercising in compassionate introspection. The shackles of guilt and self-grievance begin to fall off whilst we accept our emotions as they may be, without passing judgement.

Embracing the Present Moment with Mindfulness and Breathwork

Mindfulness and breathing sports activities offer stability inside the proper right here and now when excessive feelings threaten to weigh down. Try those techniques the subsequent time you feel an top notch wave of wrath or worry:

Sit in silence and recognition in your breathing as an exercise in aware remark. Take an objective observe the bodily sensations that pass hand in hand at the aspect of your emotions. Just classify them as "fear" or "anger" and skip on from the plot. Keep searching and letting cross.

Deep Breathing: Inhale slowly thru your nostril and exhale slowly via your mouth. Pay close to hobby to how your tummy expands as your breath fills your lungs. By triggering your parasympathetic worried machine, this clean project may also additionally assist you feel extra grounded and at peace.

When you're going via a tough emotional time, the ones strategies will will permit you to discover solace. Keep in mind that your feelings do not outline you, and that you have the strength to decide the manner to react to them.

Let Go of the Chains of Guilt and Self-Criticism

Along with our fears and rage, we regularly feel the weight of disgrace and self-blame, which keeps us mired in the beyond. We need to permit cross of these gadgets if we want to move earlier:

Exercise Response

Forgiveness Ritual Write a letter of forgiveness to your self, acknowledging your beyond mistakes and presenting unconditional self-compassion.

Burn the letter or bury it symbolically, liberating the guilt and shame connected to it.

Loving Affirmations Repeat the ones extraordinary affirmations;

I am allowed to experience my emotions" and "I am really worth of love and reputation, even though I make errors."

Remember, you aren't by myself in this adventure. Recognizing and accepting your emotions is a courageous act, and it takes time and exercising. Be moderate with yourself, have amusing your development, and accept as proper with that with every step, you're transferring in the direction of wholeness.

Diving Deeper:

Unveiling the Treasures Within the Shadow

Now that we've got surpassed through the edge of recognition, we're capable of preserve our descent into the shadows. Here, we find out the robust contraptions that may help us discover the treasures that lie dormant internal, treasures that would turn our wrath and fear into powerful partners in our trips of self-discovery.

Revealing the World of Dreams

Those hidden webs spun by using the usage of the mind within the form of dreams offer effective windows into the unknown. Those mysterious mutterings from the mind offer a gateway to the shadows' lairs. We can check hidden meanings and unearth suppressed feelings if we can parent out a way to take a look at them. Look into those dreamwork tips:

To keep a dream magazine, write down every element (pictures, feelings, locations, and so forth.) as speedy as you awaken. Consider: What message are my shadow selves trying to bring to me? If I were to dream approximately my anger or fear, who or what might not or not it's?

Study traditional dream symbols and the meanings they have as they relates for your emotional state for the purpose of symbolic evaluation. By doing so, you may be capable of discover greater profound interpretations of your goals.

Shadow Talking: Write a conversation in your magazine with a determine that stands in on your dread or rage from the dream. Inquire, show interest, and be privy to what they've got to say. Do they have got any phrases of consciousness or advice to percent?

Creativity - Into the Unknown We Step

One manner to stand our shadow in a managed setting is through energetic creativeness, a way in which we deliberately bring together inner dialogues and situations. Let your creativeness soar on those adventures:

Confronting Your Fears: Put yourself in the footwear of a person whose worst dread you may consider. How does it appear? What are your emotions approximately it? Get in contact at the side of your fear, confront it, and inform it you are decided to hold going although it is there.

Making Your Angry Feel Safe: Visualise an area in which you may vent your frustrations without fear of judgement. Pound the imaginary floor at the same time as screaming and shouting. Just watch the emotions unfold and allow them to bypass without passing judgement.

After you have were given confronted your shadow self, image it turning into a source of strength or cognizance as you integrate it into your life. How are you capable of constructively use this power into your each day existence?

As a powerful tool for introspection, mirror artwork enables us to have a look at our subconscious feelings pondered in our very very own picture. Get within the the front of a mirror and bear in mind the following questions:

Reflecting Feelings: Show your dread or rage thru your frame language and facial expressions. Pay attention to the feelings and reviews that rise up. With no criticism, are you capable of encompass those factors of your man or woman?

Shadow Dialogue: Facing the replicate, have a verbal exchange together together with your shadow self. Inquire as to its dreams, needs, anxieties, and dreams. Would you be able to reply with empathy and compassion?

Positive Self-Talk inside the Mirror: While staring into your own eyes, say matters such, "I am really worth of affection and popularity, even though I battle with worry and anger." A new story of self-reputation and compassion can be born from this.

Expressing Oneself Creatively: Freeing the Unbridled Spirit

Words can not always particular how we truly sense. When it entails digesting and addressing the shadow, innovative expression is a sturdy tool:

Art in Motion is right here: Let your feelings out in some thing revolutionary way you need—dance, portray, sculpting, and plenty of others. Forget approximately looking for to be best; as an opportunity, have a observe the lead of your shadow self.

Musical Experiments: Express your anger or tension thru making a song, gambling an device, or creating a soundscape. Find out more about your inner global by using the usage of paying attention to the tune you're making.

Using Vulnerability in Writing: Use your shadow as a narrator in a piece of poetry, prose, or magazine writing. No one should be capable of silence it because it expresses its private thoughts, desires, and fears.

Do now not forget about that there may be more than one correct technique for shadowing. Discover what speaks for your man or woman inner international by the usage of manner of experimenting and exploring. As you delve farther, believe that the shadows cover precious gemstones - power, imagination, and a more profound comprehension of your non-public identity.

In order to help readers face and integrate their shadow aspects, it gives journaling prompts and particular wearing activities for every approach. In the following economic wreck, the emphasis moves to embracing one's converted self and living a existence empowered thru wholeness; this bankruptcy gadgets the framework for that.

Chapter 10: Facing Triggers

This is wherein the course of shadow paintings makes a dramatic U-switch on this segment. Here we are on the intersection of our inner demons and the outside factors that could set off the explosive mix of feelings this is our personal rage and dread. In this region, we gain the potential to traverse this unpredictable panorama, no longer helpless patients of our emotional reactions however rather powerful commanders of them.

Embedded in the Darkness

Unexpected criticism or a site site visitors congestion are examples of outdoor occurrences that could feature hooks, catching the strands of our dormant feelings and troubles. If you have ever skilled rejection as a infant, taking a public speaking opportunity may want to carry lower lower back terrible degree anxiety.

Triggers might also seem as outside influences, however they'll be definitely opportunities to stand your dark aspect, listen to its murmurs, and reply with self-attention.

The Dance of the Shadow

Realizing that triggers are lurking at some point of the corner is the first step toward managing them. Pay attention to:

Mood Swings: Pay interest to unexpected adjustments for your mood, which encompass an escalation of anxiety or a buildup of rage, mainly in instances that don't appear to warrant them. Even despite the fact that the ones changes are small, they suggest that the shadow is dancing.

Feelings inside the Body: Anxiety, e.G racing coronary coronary heart, clinched hands, or tightness of the chest. As warning symptoms of an drawing near motive activation, the ones physiological responses frequently rise up earlier than emotional outbursts.

Vacuous thoughts: Pay hobby to the story that develops inner of you at the same time as wonderful activities arise. Can you inform if it is critical, accusatory, or catastrophic? In order to interrupt free from the shadow's grip, it's far critical to perceive nice concept styles.

Practicing Mindfulness-Based Responses Instead of Reactivity

After we've got diagnosed them, triggers do not want to manipulate our conduct. Some techniques to reply mindfully are as follows:

Take an prolonged breath outside and inside to centre yourself inside the here and now in advance than responding. The autopilot mode is disrupted and aware desire is made possible via this simple act.

Keep an Open Mind: Witness your feelings with out allowing them to sweep you away. Identify them as "fear" or "anger" without passing judgement, recognising their life without letting them manipulate your reactions.

Change the Storyline: Put an save you to the awful strategies of thinking that the condition has brought approximately. Consider this: "Is this case truely as threatening as my thoughts is making it out to be?" Is there a actually one in every of a kind manner to have a examine it that could provide you with extra manipulate?

Reflecting at the Past, Reimagining the Future

A sturdy method for identifying triggers and developing greater wholesome coping structures is reflected picture. Some examples of journaling turns on are: Think all over again on a time even as you had an undesirable response to a purpose. Tell me what set it off. What changed into your reaction? How did your response play out in the long run?

Picture yourself within the future encountering the equal trigger. Instead of responding on impulse, what healthy techniques of coping with strain may additionally additionally you appoint? Using mindfulness and self-compassion, jot down a whole method for handling the scenario.

Keep in mind that managing triggers does not entail disposing of them in fact. Instead of letting them be emotional landmines, you may learn how to reply with aware preference, to be able to result in non-public boom and mastery.

In this journey's final financial ruin, we can enjoy the electricity of embracing the shadow and its remodeling electricity, power and tenacity. Pay interest, for a number of the shadows can be located a terrific slight, and also you, my friend, are the most effective who may find out it.

The Alchemy of Fear

Here we are, on the brink of trade, in which we are in a function to turn the dread of the unknown into an elixir of power, dedication, and manage over our non-public lives. In the destiny, fear will not be a stifling force but instead a lighthouse warning us of peril in the shadows of our aspirations. In this lesson, we can find out the way to faucet into its latent strengths and turn its worry into the courage to take ambitious, assured steps in advance.

Fear: A Friend, Not an Enemy

There has been a protracted-reputation tendency to stable worry as an antagonist in our lives, some thing we must try and exchange. However, what if we modified our perspective and observed fear as a honest, if demanding, partner in choice to a terrifying foe? Ultimately, worry serves as a primitive caution tool, a watchful father or mother ensuring our safety. It warns of imminent danger, encourages us to be geared up for everything, and lights the fuse of unique self-maintenance.

Shifting from Fear to Triumph

What are we able to do, therefore, to reveal this dread into power and bravery? Here are a few powerful alchemical techniques:

Revealing the Hidden Message: Pay hobby to the cries of terror. Can you decipher its message? Is it warning of a actual hazard, pleading for prudence, or absolutely expressing uncertainty? We can decipher the real meaning of worry and act correctly if we recognize in which it comes from.

You can not positioned out the hearth of fear thru fending off it. Go as an opportunity into the fiery pit of your fears. Recreate your fear in secure, controlled settings with the useful resource of manner of revealing yourself to subjects that make you involved. Take a step in the direction of conquering your imagined "monster" with the aid of attending public talking seminars, a mountaineering gymnasium for acrophobia, or an open mic night time time for degree fright. With each step, your fears will decrease and your talents will increase.

Bold Proclamations: Use powerful affirmations to counter the horrible reminiscences that fear tells you. "I am brave," "I am succesful," "I face stressful conditions with resilience." Like incantations, repeat those mantras till you trust to your functionality to triumph over obstacles.

A Tale of Flying Through the Air

There are infinite recollections in information of individuals who overcame worry and flew to exquisite heights, from Amelia Earhart soaring via the heavens to Nelson Mandela resisting an oppressive authorities. If you're searching out inspiration to push yourself beyond your consolation sector and overcome your issues, the ones reminiscences ought to feature a beacon.

www.ingramcontent.com/pod-product-compliance
Lightning Source LLC
Chambersburg PA
CBHW070118110526
44587CB00014BA/2016